THE
BIG WILDERNESS
CANOE
Manual

THE BIG WILDERNESS CANOE Manual

BOB CARY

ARCO PUBLISHING, INC.
NEW YORK

This book is dedicated to my wife Lil, who has paddled and portaged over a good hunk of North America with me over the past years and has outfished me nearly every mile of the way.

First Arco Edition, First Printing, 1983

Published by Arco Publishing, Inc.
215 Park Avenue South, New York, N.Y. 10003

Library of Congress Cataloging in Publication Data

Cary, Bob.
  The big wilderness canoe manual.

  1. Canoes and canoeing. I. Title.
GV783.C33 1983   797.1'22   83-8729
ISBN 0-668-05847-1 (Cloth Edition)

Printed in the United States of America

833989

Most of what I may have learned about canoe camping during the last half century I have learned from professional guides, trappers, hunters, anglers, canoe racers, canoe designers and builders, bush pilots, and outfitters. This, in a very real sense, is their book, and I hope the information it contains will make your trips as enjoyable as it has made mine.

Bob Cary
Ely, Minnesota

Contents

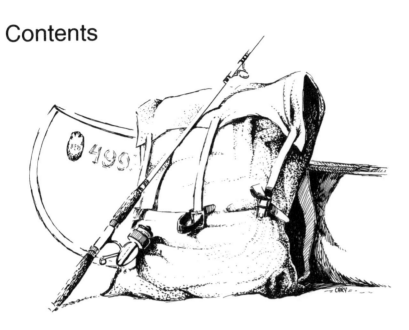

Chapter 1

The Invisible Canoeman

Between the frothy thunder of Chatterton Falls and
the granite-walled silence of Sturgeon Narrows on
the headwaters of Ontario's Maligne River lies a
pine-shaded campsite where the slick current curls along the north
shore, a spot favored by generations of travelers in the Quetico-
Superior canoe country.

It was a warm evening in July as we drove the bow of our canoe
into the eddy by the campsite, beached, and stepped out.

"Somebody just left here," my wife Lil said.

If she inherited anything from her Cherokee great-grand-
mother, it was a sharp set of eyes. I followed her gaze from the
trees to the shore as it swiftly catalogued the signs of occupation:
the outline of a tent carved into the needle-carpeted turf, a
shallow, rectangular trench for carrying off excess rainfall; a pole
frame wired together and containing a carefully laid bed of

balsam tips; tent poles, freshly cut and trimmed, leaning against the bole of a massive Norway pine; peeled and sharpened tent pegs stacked neatly below the poles; a built-up rock fireplace topped by a big smoke-blackened grate, converted from a section of old refrigerator shelf; a stack of split kindling protected by a square of plastic sheeting held in place by a rock on each corner; two dry, ten-inch logs ready to be sawed and split; a piece of soap on a flat rock near the water's edge.

Not a scrap of paper, aluminum foil, or cigarette butt was anywhere in sight. If those departed campers had been attending an outdoor school in modern camping, they would have received high marks for cleanliness, but they would still have flunked the course.

In order, Lil and I set about repairing the damage. First, we carefully replaced the turf chipped out of the trench. We unwired the bed frame, coiled the wire and set it aside, then picked up all of the balsam tips and scattered them way back in the forest. Next we took the bed poles, tent poles, and peeled stakes, along with the two ten-inch logs, and shoved them into the underbrush two hundred feet from the campsite. The impressive fireplace was reduced to a few essential rocks, the rest replaced along the shore, whence they had originated. The residue from seasons of camp-fires was scraped into the plastic sheet, the charcoal picked out and stacked by the split wood, the ashes removed to the forest and sprinkled into the understory. Finally, the smoked grate was folded over, stamped flat, rolled up in the plastic bag along with the soap and wire, and shoved into a packsack to be hauled out.

With the campsite somewhat near normal, we pitched our lightweight, aluminum-poled nylon tent, stowed foam mats and sleeping bags inside, unpacked our small camping grate from its denim cover, leveled it on the half-dozen remaining rocks and, with a few sticks and leftover charcoal, cooked supper. We were following as closely as possible today's concept of the invisible canoeist: the waterborne camper who makes so little impact that it cannot be readily determined whether he passed by yesterday, last week, or last year. It is similar to a slogan used in the Boy Scout High Adventure program: "Take only pictures, leave only footprints," and a cousin to the high-country backpacker's theme from the Appalachians to the Sierras: to wipe out all possible in-dication of campsite occupancy. It is an idea whose time, of neces-sity, has come.

The Maligne River campsite exemplified many of the problems encountered today in canoe-country travel. Though our efforts to remove signs of heavy tenancy might have brought more than one snort of derision from old-time paddle pushers, there were some practical aspects perhaps not immediately apparent.

First, it is against Ontario law, as applied to parks, to cut live trees for any purpose. Had an Ontario ranger dropped in on us for tea, we would have had an embarrassing time trying to explain how those freshly cut balsam boughs, tent poles, and peeled pegs happened to be on our campsite. Had we been using any of them, there would have been a clear indication they were ours, and we could have been subject to arrest and a fine. On the U.S. side of the border, regulations are equally strict; anyone hacking down live saplings for any purpose had better have a valid logging permit.

Furthermore, only bulky, heavy, old-style duck tents require a wooden frame and ridgepole. Modern, lightweight tents with sewn-in floors and mosquito screens come equipped with jointed aluminum poles and light metal pegs. They are more easily erected, decidedly better ventilated, drier, and a lot more comfortable than the old-style tents, whether you are inside them or they are inside your backpack.

It takes a couple of hours to construct a good balsam bed, even where such activity might be legal; it takes seconds to unroll a comfortable foam mat. And the foam mat doesn't deposit drops of sticky pitch on tent floors and sleeping bags.

Digging a drainage canal around the outside of a tent is a throwback to the days of canvas shelters without sewn-in floors. The theory was that the ditch (some looked like a moat) would collect and carry off excess rainwater like the gutters on a house roof. In practice, the ditch usually filled quickly with water and overflowed, and the water went where it would have gone anyway, through one corner of the tent and out the other. If the site was not carefully selected, this flow could vary in volume from a trickle to a tidal wave.

In much of the northern canoe country, soils are thin and trenching can quickly start erosion, reducing a good tent site to bare rock in a season or two. New tent designs incorporate sewn-in, waterproof floors that lap up several inches on the sides, front, and back; coupled with waterproof rain-flies that extend beyond the eaves on all sides, such a tent makes it nearly impossible for you to get wet. Also, to make a trench requires the use of a small shovel or an axe. If the axe is used for ditching, it is obvious the camper doesn't have much regard for the edge of his blade.

A tent erected in one place for more than one night can adversely shade and impact a normal surface, which could, over a few seasons, start an erosion problem. An alternative, in good weather, is to unstake the front, back, and one side of the tent, loop the guy ropes through the peg loops, and tie them to overhanging branches so air and light can circulate under the tent as the floor is raised. This practice has the added benefit of drying out any dampness that may have crept into the floor during the night. Metal pegs are light and compact, hold better in a variety of situations, and do not require any whittling.

Huge rock fireplaces may save a little bending or stooping, and they offer a challenge to neophyte stonemasons, but they are not worth much as wilderness kitchen ranges. A small fire grate balanced about eight inches off the ground will accommodate an easily controlled cooking fire that will do a much better job with a fraction of the wood. Such a fireplace is quite mobile and can be moved around to accommodate shifts in wind and weather. With the small fire, there is no need to buck up and split logs for kindling. A small stack of thumb-thick sticks will handle the job quite well.

In northern Minnesota's Boundary Waters Canoe Area, the U.S. Forest Service has installed permanent cast-iron grates on hundreds of designated campsites in order to confine fires to designated places and restrict their size. The 14 x 28 grates are anchored in rock or gravel and are excellent from a fire safety standpoint since they are placed on a nonburnable surface well away from roots, stumps, or overhanging conifers. Designated campsites with specifically located fireplaces became a necessity as increasing numbers of poorly educated or miseducated campers began building fires on the porous duff in the forest, fires that often appeared to be out, but which burned underground for a day or a week and then popped up to consume a campsite, an island, or a section of wooded shoreline. From the standpoint of cooking, the grates are larger than needed for most camps, but will handle groups. Also, they are set too high off the ground. Forest Service crews found that if they set the grates at a good low level for cooking, some campers would use logs to pry the grates up to a twelve- or eighteen-inch height. As a result, they set them purposely high so the amateur who wants to prepare his meals over a raging inferno has that option, and the expert who wishes to cook on a small fire may build up the fire bed to correct height with a few flat rocks.

Designated campsites in the BWCA also have built-in, low-level wooden biffies that many canoeists believe (and correctly) detract from the wilderness concept. The Forest Service should not be faulted on these facilities, however. Prior to their installation on the more popular canoe routes, some campers' unorganized methods of coping with bowel problems rendered the shady portions of many campsites as hazardous to cross as a cattle feedlot—and just as smelly and fly-ridden. Most experienced campers know how to locate a biffy site, lash up a pole or two for a "seat," and kick down a few inches into the duff for a hole, setting aside the turf to be replaced when the party breaks camp. The uninitiated, however, often simply backed up to a tree, nailed logs between trees and even cut down live trees to hang their tails over—and left wads of varicolored toilet paper to decorate the shrubbery at the whim of prevailing winds.

The drawback to the dug biffy is that human wastes do not rapidly decompose in the holes, but the Forest Service does not yet have an alternative until all campers learn the elements of wilderness sanitation. With designated campsites, equipped with a fire grate and biffy, the forest managers also have the option of closing an overused site, allowing it to regenerate, and opening an alternate site somewhere in the same vicinity.

Beginning in 1976, quotas were set for the number of canoeists who could enter any access point at one time between June 1 and Labor Day in the Boundary Waters area. Though the method of assigning canoe campers to routes under these quotas has been a source of debate between Forest Service personnel, outfitters, guides, and campers, the idea of dispersing canoeists from the heavily used routes to more remote and less-visited areas is readily accepted. Ontario's Algonquin Park (one of the most popular eastern wilderness areas) and Quetico Park have gone to the quota system. Quotas are an attempt to reduce impact. A reduction of impact need not necessarily mean a reduction of the number of canoeists. Present or even increased numbers of canoeists can use the water routes if impact is minimized by adoption of the canoe camping ethic. This needs widespread advertising.

Unfortunately, most of the current outdoor-use advertising is aimed at increasing impact and is eminently successful in doing that. One must stand in awe of the selling genius of those manufacturers of plastic products who have managed to convince a large segment of the camping public that polyethylene film is the final word in tents, tarps, ground cloths, windbreaks, and kitchen flies. "A thousand uses," the pitch goes. It is relatively inexpensive too, as testified to by the dozens of plastic film housing developments abandoned each summer along North American canoe routes. Sheet plastic is lightweight, waterproof, and easy to haul in for a one-time camp. Unfortunately, few people care to fold it up and haul it back out—that is, with the exception of those guides, dedicated campers, and forestry personnel who are continually cleaning up other people's messes.

Polyethylene has several excellent uses in wilderness camping: as food bags, waterproof clothing bags, sleeping bag containers, trash bags, and map covers. But it is a pain in the neck when used as a shelter. Manufacturers who advertise plastic film for outdoor use should be required to stamp it with large, easily read words to the effect: "This product is not biodegradable. If you do not intend to pack it out of the woods, do not purchase it and take it in." Wilderness campsites do not need to be improved by any red, black, green, orange, or clear plastic streamers waving in the wind from pole frames. Nor is there a critical need for any more pillow-sized globs of semimelted plastic where campers attempted to burn their shiny shelters in the cook fire.

At the Maligne River campsite, that piece of soap we picked up and packed out with the sheet of plastic was not a great environmental disaster in itself, but it indicated two common camping practices that need to be quickly discouraged: doing dishes on the shoreline, and taking a bath in the lake or river. Only the rank amateur any longer uses the recreational waterways for his kitchen sink or bathtub. Dishes, as well as body scrubbing, are better done well up on the campsite where the soapy water can be emptied into the underbrush to be consumed by plant and animal life. Dishwater, particularly, should be taken well back into the woods so that bits of food do not attract animals or insects to your campsite. Cooking sites where dishwater has been regularly used to douse fires are quite often garrisoned by legions of biting flies.

Aquatic biologists point out that all lakes and rivers are subject to a phenomenon called eutrophication, which is no more than a ritzy word for aging. Aging is caused by a buildup of solids in a water system, which eventually results in a filled-in, overgrown basin. Most of the muskeg bogs in the northland were once lakes that filled, over centuries, with leaves, branches, roots, and sediment until they would support a plant cover. Nutrients, such as bird and animal wastes, dying aquatic life, and chemical leaching from ground sources, hasten eutrophication. Algae "blooms," symptoms of nutrient-rich waters, are common in waterways near intensively developed recreation centers, urban, and industrial areas. Such blooms are also appearing in some of the wilderness areas, and though there is a high phosphorus count in some watersheds, it is suspected that soap and detergents are contributing a share. Longtime use of North America's wilderness areas decrees as little human impact as possible. This decree includes the complete elimination of soaps from the water.

Fortunately, on that Quetico campsite I mentioned at the outset, there were no cans, bottles, foil, or other trash. Cans and bottles have all but disappeared from the Quetico-Superior canoe area after adoption of a no-can, no-bottle food-outfitting program initiated by Northern Minnesota Canoe Outfitters and adopted by the U.S. Forest Service in 1968 for the Boundary Waters Canoe Area. At the same time, the State of Minnesota adopted similar regulations on lands and waters under its jurisdiction within the BWCA. Under these laws, no one is allowed to take food or beverages into the 2,000-square-mile BWCA in nonburnable containers except containers that are normally refillable, such as Thermos bottles.

Two considerations gave birth to this idea: First, can and bottle trash on campsites had reached epidemic proportions prior to 1967, requiring yearly expenditures of $90,000 for canoe trail cleanup crews; second, processors of specialized camping food had developed adequate, tasty dehydrated and freeze-dried foods packed in burnable or easily removed pouches. Outfitters had long used plastic jars and plastic bottles for repacking such items as cooking oil, oleo, peanut butter, and jam. Within one season after official adoption of the no-can, no-bottle regulations, that type of litter vanished. It has not come back.

An educational side effect of the throwaway ban has been a general increase in impact awareness by the campers. Not only did canoeists quickly adjust to the new rules, but they also appeared to become generally more tidy and less destructive as the campsites became progressively cleaner. There are still some green saplings being cut for tent poles and even firewood, and a few birches are skinned out piecemeal by amateur nature lovers who wish to take a token of their love home with them. But this type of damage in ratio to the number of campers has declined.

Some trail foods, of course, come in foil pouches. Empty pouches, spread single-layer on a hot fire, will usually oxidize to ash. Or they can be packed out in the trash bag, contributing no significant weight or bulk. Plastic jars with snap-on lids are burnable, but most campers wash them out and reuse them. With care, they will make several trips.

Many canoeists have dispensed with the open fire entirely, preferring to go with small trail stoves. Light, compact, fuel-efficient backpackers' stoves were quickly adopted by canoeists as they became available. Stove cooking naturally eliminates the need for wood cutting, and the weight of the burner and fuel are offset by the elimination of axe or saw. Quick ignition, regardless of weather conditions, is an additional stove advantage. Most veteran campers prefer liquid-fuel stoves over the bottled-gas variety for canoe use. Bottled gas is bulky, and there is a tendency to abandon empty containers rather than pack them out. Until there is a deposit on the bottles or all of them are rechargeable, there is a considerable sentiment among many wilderness travelers that bottled-gas stoves are best relegated to use on highly developed federal, state, county, and private campgrounds where daily garbage collection is available.

Fortunately, there is still ample firewood along most of the major canoe routes in North America, a perpetually renewable fuel supply as long as campers keep fires small, use only what they need for cooking, and avoid such wood-wasting activities as the group "bonfire" for late night sing-a-long sessions.

Groups, in themselves, pose a problem. During the past decade, the size of groups using the canoe routes and the impact of these groups have come under scrutiny by both U.S. and Canadian forest personnel. A study under U.S. Forest Service auspices, completed in 1970, showed that the most significant adverse impact on the Boundary Waters area was from large groups of paddlers. This conclusion confirmed what guides had asserted for years: when twenty, thirty, or forty people assemble on one campsite to sleep, cook, and socialize, the drain on firewood, the impact from clearing tent sites, and the soil impaction from just that many feet pounding on the grass and duff often leave the area looking like an abandoned battleground. In the Boundary Waters Canoe Area, group size has been limited by law to ten persons on one campsite at any time. Some private summer camps have set up a quota of nine using three canoes with three persons and duffle to each canoe and two tents to each campsite. In addition, most of the organized private camps have intensive educational programs, lasting from one to several days prior to the actual canoe trip, insuring close supervision and a continuation of the educational program enroute.

Independent wilderness guides hired by individuals and groups through commercial canoe outfitters generally have a considerable regard for the area they work in. These guides constitute one-man campsite and portage trail cleanup crews and are constantly vigilant in spotting and dousing other campers' abandoned and still-smoldering cook fires. They are also in the business of educating and supervising the activities of the people they guide.

To better instruct those canoeists who arrive at access points with their own equipment and food, Canadian and U.S. foresters provide programs and materials aimed at instructing these voyageurs in low-impact camping. Currently in use are filmstrips, tape recordings, displays of camp setups, posters, photo displays, pamphlets, and lists of rules. It is recognized, however, that it is difficult for a neophyte camper to absorb much of this material prior to his trip, since he has little background with which to relate to it. Some outfitters, just at the start of a trip, provide illustrated pocket folders with the essentials of good camping procedure for clients to take along on their trips.

You may hear considerable criticism from old-timers about how the inexperienced newcomers are desecrating the waterways, but not all of the problems are associated with young campers. Many of the younger generation have a high environmental awareness and are quick to absorb much of the outdoor idealism found in the pages of magazines specializing in wilderness living. A camp leader or guide finds it much easier to instruct an eager youngster in good woods manners than old retreads who have been doing the same wrong things on the waterways for several decades. Unfortunately, both inexperienced and old-time campers are being assaulted with many books, magazine articles, and newspaper columns containing that same old discredited, high-impact campercraft so dear to the hearts of outdoorsmen in grandfather's era. The worst are the books.

There are hundreds of thousands of books sold annually that advocate camping practices that are obsolete at best, illegal or dangerous at worst. If such out-of-date books were printed as historical items with a preface stating that the information therein should be read in the context of an outdoors that existed some 40 or 50 years ago, the effect would not be so damaging. Many of these books, however, are marketed as the last word in modern canoe camping procedure, often coming out as "new" or "revised" versions of earlier encyclopedias of misinformation.

The experienced canoeist, tuned into the low-impact camping trend, immediately recognizes the same old rehash of errors one writer picks up from an earlier one, which gives the reader the uncomfortable feeling that maybe the author didn't really try some of the practices described, or if he did, only briefly. Some publications are not much more than equipment catalogues. Canoeists accepting this type of advice are readily visible on the portages, busy moving a mountain of gear from one landing to another. On the water, they look like crewmen guiding a New York City garbage scow.

It is nearly impossible to pick up a camping book without running into detailed descriptions on how to build a whole spectrum of fires, from roaring pyramids to pyres augmented with built-up log "reflectors," all of which consume stacks of wood, and none of which are any good to cook on. There are diagrams showing how to drive forked limbs into the ground to support a ridgepole over the fire, from which pots are hung with all manner of whittled-out pothooks. Instructions are included on how to construct camp furniture, including bough beds, and how to dig a hole into the ground for cooking and even to heat a tent. Axes and saws get a share of attention with illustrations of various types of bucksaws and chopping tools, usually with a full-page photo of somebody whacking up a log, the caption reading, "Proper Stance for Chopping."

The mounds of wood chips and segments of partially chopped logs found on some campsites are testimony that campers, as a group, are literate. Sometimes there is even a debate over the merits of the single-bit versus the double-bit axe, as though the canoeist were going to hack a four-lane right-of-way through the forest. All the dry wood two people can use in a trip can be broken with the hands or leaned against a ledge and cracked with the boot sole. For a group, a small pruning saw is worth more than an axe although a lightweight hand axe could help with any necessary splitting. There has been serious consideration among the managers of some U.S. wilderness areas of eliminating the use of axes altogether as a means of eliminating campsite damage. There is no doubt that much of the axemanship being illustrated in many outdoor books is also being tested on pines, spruce, fir, and hardwoods along the continent's canoe trails.

Other types of camp tools get a fair share of attention, also. Sheath knives, some of cleaver proportions, are described with tips on selecting one with a good edge. A good edge for what is rarely explained. Sheath knives are a throwback to frontier days when a belt weapon was considered an aid if your gun jammed. Unquestionably, many disagreements arise among canoe campers, but few serious enough to warrant a knife fight. The only long-bladed knife with utility value is a thin, flexible fillet knife, which is most easily carried in the food pack until needed. A good pocketknife will do about all of the cutting a canoeist is likely to require.

In the shelter category, you can find recommendations for a variety of outmoded designs including the bulky, open-end, dirt floor Baker tent. This canvas disaster is simply a box with the front missing, and its description is usually accompanied by the suggestion, "If you are in insect country, you may wish to carry a separate mosquito tent that ties inside the Baker tent at the corners." *If* you are in insect country? There may be some watersheds in North America where mosquitos do not breed, but few canoeists have seen them.

Another "advantage" of the Baker tent is warmth. That is, a fire can be built in front that reflects inside, keeping the occupants "warm as toast." The idea here is that if your sleeping bags are inadequate, somebody in the party will get up periodically during the night to feed the fire. Sure he will.

There are still some silly or illegal practices in print, such as instructions on how to put all the nonburnables in a bag, weight it with a rock, and sink it in the middle of the lake. Or dig a garbage pit behind the campsite for bottles, cans, and food scraps—which is fine if the object of the trip is to bait a bear within spearing distance.

With all this literary fertilizer being distributed, there is quite often a chapter or two on "modern additions" to the camping scene, including the use of aluminum foil. It is about as essential to have aluminum foil on a wilderness canoe trip as having an electric toothbrush. Yet some books have photos illustrating methods of making foil pots "that you can really cook with," foil cups, foil pans—as if the camper is so dumb he is likely to forget his cook kit but remember to bring his roll of aluminum foil. Like sheet plastic, aluminum foil easily migrates into the wilderness but is reluctant to leave. Thus campers are forever finding bits of foil, balls of foil, and folded sheets of foil artistically tucked between rocks and in the ashes of campsite cooking areas.

Along with producing the flurry of literary endeavor, the camping boom has also spawned a host of fringe industries that are deluging the public with mounds of junk such as throwaway tents, throwaway sleeping bags, throwaway cigarette lighters, throwaway raincoats, and other paraphernalia to match throwaway food and beverage containers. At a campsite on Ontario's Turtle River, some fifty miles from nowhere, we found the chrome frames of two folding lawn chairs, apparently abandoned when the webbed seats gave out. It is an incongruity of the time that some people who take to the outdoors to escape the complexities of mechanized urban life wind up carrying as much of that urban life as their backs can stand. Occasionally, on very remote canoe-country lakes, you will discover wilderness travelers who have taken off two weeks and spent upwards of $500 apiece to escape the city, listening to the evening news on a portable radio, afraid they may have missed something. There is hardly a guide left in the north country who hasn't, at one time or another, run across campers attempting to drown out the sounds of the forest with rock music on a portable tape player.

Some of these campers who move piles of gear with them are neat, clean campers. But there is always the possibility that those additional luxuries may break, tear, spring a leak, or fall apart, followed by abandonment.

Just how much equipment constitutes necessity? Canoe outfitters who specialize in lightweight trips figure a canoe and two packsacks for two people is a normal load. One pack contains food, the other contains equipment. Whoever portages the canoe carries the lighter pack with the sleeping bags, mats, and tents. This arrangement leaves the food pack and any loose gear for his companion and makes it possible to cross any portage in a single trip.

The Ontario Ministry of Natural Resources recently came out with a series of antilitter posters bearing the message, "There's no maid service here"—indicating that campers must accept the responsibility of picking up after themselves. Canoeists who pack "close," that is, go with only essential gear, have nothing to throw away. Furthermore, they travel lighter and faster and are less fatigued at the end of the day.

The buckskin forerunners of today's paddlers were experts at low-impact camping. One reason they left no sign of their passing was that someone not steeped in fraternal affection might be following them. As they traveled swiftly and silently up the rivers and across the lakes, they were, indeed, the invisible canoemen.

It is an ideal worthy of pursuit.

Chapter 2

Canots du Nord

The Anishinabe, the "Good People" whom we know as our Ojibwa neighbors, called their birchbark craft by the name "Gee-maun." Had these skilled designers of shallow-draft boats felt a compelling need for a written language some four centuries ago, we might now be calling our paddle craft Gee-maun instead of "canoe."

Spanish sailors who first dropped anchor in the Caribbean applied the term "canoa" to native dugout craft. It was subsequently used for all of the open bark boats in North America, the French spelling the name "canaux" or "canot." For three centuries the Canot du Nord, or North Canoe, was the backbone of the continental fur trade, Scotch-English traders anglicizing the spelling to the current "canoe."

Thus the name of the craft is no more accurate than "Indian" is the correct name for the original residents, a blunder by European sailors who incorrectly assumed they had landed in the East Indies, a slight navigational error of some 12,000 miles. But "canoe" has been around so long that even the Anishinabe and their brothers west, north, and east use the term—except when talking among themselves.

Of course, everybody knows what a canoe is. Until he goes to define it. Not even Webster has been able to come up with an accurate definition. Most North Americans would say it is a light, shallow-draft, rounded-bottom hull that can be propelled by hand. And perhaps it is just as well to let it go at that. Unquestionably, the native American developed a near-perfect displacement-hull design for hand power. He also provided a love and feeling of kinship for his craft that has persisted to this day.

Auk-yeh-fesheek-yawnup, "The Man Who Came from the North Star," a sixth-generation Ojibwa medicine man, once told me: "Our people treated a canoe gently, like a woman. And like a woman, it responded to their every need." As a boy on Rainy Lake, decades ago, he recalls seeing his father, Pee-nah-wawn-say, "The Falling Snowflake," constructing bark canoes with other tribal craftsmen. With no written instructions, no scale drawings to refer to, this was a feat requiring not only extraordinary dexterity but considerable mental concentration. Each dimension and process had to be memorized from the first slice of a quartz knife on a living birch tree to the final touch of pitch on the spruce-root lacing.

Historians of European descent tend to describe the bark canoe as "rough" or "crude." But it was neither. Only the tools were rough or crude. The finished craft was precisely and artistically engineered, its length, beam, depth, and capacity designed for a specific use. The red man thoroughly understood the value of a "V" bow entry and stern exit, the use of rocker to improve seaworthiness and maneuverability, tumblehome for buoyancy, and stress to provide strength and tautness. Laminations for maintaining strength on curved members were standard on gunwale strips and stem pieces. Native bark craft I have studied and photographed, although dating from only the middle and late 1800s, show hull variations from narrow, round-bottom racing styles, 15' 3" long, to wide, deep freighters. Indeed, there is very little that is "new" in today's canoe design. Improvements have been in tools and materials. Any serious canoeist interested in the ancestors of his modern craft will find a superb collection of information in "Bark Canoes and Skin Boats of North America," Bulletin 230 of the Smithsonian Institution, written by Howard I. Chapelle, Curator of Transportation. Chapelle correlated a mass of material gathered by the late E. T. Adney, the foremost U.S.

authority on bark canoes, and added a wealth of his own studies on skin boats.

The first "European" canoe factory was established in the 1700s at Trois Riviere, near Montreal, turning out birchbark trade craft with an overall length of 30 feet or more, depth of 26 inches, a five-foot beam, and a capacity of four tons, including a crew of eight. The same factory also built express canoes, 21 feet or shorter, with a four-foot beam, for quick trips to the backcountry. There is a mistaken idea that these were big, clumsy designs hardly comparable to sleek, modern craft. Not so. With a full crew, they fairly flew over the water. They still do.

One of the most knowledgeable authorities on the North Canoe of the voyageurs is designer Ralph Frese, who operates his unique Chicagoland Canoe Base on Narragansett Avenue, almost in the shadow of Chicago's Loop. Ralph has made a business-hobby out of reproducing authentic copies of the original craft, only substituting a fiberglass skin for unobtainable birchbark. The 1976 LaSalle Expedition, retracing the explorers' 1680 route from Montreal to New Orleans, used six of these craft, built with hand-split cedar planking, ribs of split white cedar, and pegged with wood. He also makes all-fiberglass models much in demand by youth camps.

Bark canoes were in use up until the early 1900s by the Hudson Bay Company, when the last Indian-built craft were replaced by wood and canvas. In an era when recreational canoeists haul perhaps 50 to 70 pounds on their backs and consider 20 to 30 miles per day a good paddle distance, it might be well to reflect on the 50-miles-per-day average of the Montreal fur traders who ordinarily packed several 200-pound bales of trade goods over each portage.

Oddly enough, there are no reliable records on the origin of wood-and-canvas canoes. Of a certainty, they were first fabricated by eastern boat builders, men who perceived the advantage of laying a smooth, durable cover over a prebuilt wooden hull, rather than forcing the planking and ribs inside the skin as with bark construction. There were canvas canoes built at Peterborough, Ontario, in the 1880s, and at Old Town, Maine, about the same time. The Old Town Company, a consolidation of several builders, occurred in 1902. Wood and canvas had its heyday for the next four decades with no indication that there could be any possible improvement. But the minds of boat builders are never idle.

In 1945, the Grumman Aircraft Company found itself suddenly without a war and with a large surplus of tempered aluminum, machinery, and skilled craftsmen. The first Grumman canoe rolled off the line at Bethpage, Long Island, that year, ushering in what might be termed the modern era of canoeing.

It took North American outdoorsmen, guides, and outfitters only one ride to see the advantages of a tough, reasonably priced, maintenance-free canoe, making up in lightness what it may have lost in speed. From that beginning came the whole epoch of metal, fiberglass, plastic, and wood-strip construction that provided the impetus for the current burgeoning interest in cruising and white-water sport.

Fiberglass provided, initially, an easily formed material that could be fabricated in anybody's basement or garage, spawning a host of designs from paddlers who could not find the lines they sought in established commercial hulls. With the renaissance in shape came a proliferation of manufacturers, more than a hundred in North America, each insisting he offers the fastest, safest, lightest, mostest canoe in the world—all of which appears somewhat baffling to the camper who seeks a good cruising hull.

Essentially, what all this leads up to is that there just ain't no all-around "best" canoe design; there are only canoes for different types of water and different uses, a conclusion the original residents of this continent came to centuries ago. The question facing the canoe buyer is where he is going to do most of his canoeing. Notice that qualification, "most." Canoes are quite adaptable, within limits, and most canoes can be used reasonably well on a variety of waters. Some just work better than others.

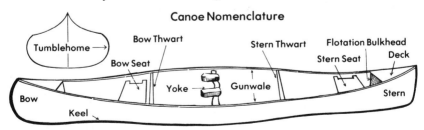

Canoe Nomenclature

First, it should be understood what a canoe hull does in the water. As a "displacement hull," a canoe replaces the same weight of water as the sum of its weight plus load. Just how it displaces that water determines how it handles.

A canoe is propelled when the bow and stern men lean ahead, put their blades in the water, and pull back—in essence "pulling" the canoe ahead. As the canoe moves, the bow splits the water, which is pushed away from the hull, then reforms behind. The smoother this movement is accomplished, the faster the craft travels, and the less effort is required. Smoothness is determined by the shape of the canoe and the amount of hull surface that touches the water. For the camping cruiser, hull shape is modified for stability, buoyancy, ease of steering, and portability.

What might be called the "traditional" design—fairly high bow and stern, wide beam, flattened bottom, ample tumblehome, full-length fin keel, and high seats—is the most commonly found at youth camps, outfitters, and liveries. Because the market has been largest for this type of craft, most manufacturers followed the trend. And this is what is mostly sold by department-store clerks whose canoe knowledge consists in running a hand over a sleek gunwale and murmuring, "Isn't it beautiful?"

In marine specialty shops, you're more apt to find proprietors who are also canoeists, people who will inquire about your intended use of the canoe and will then try to fit the need.

In the overall picture, however, it is only with experience that a canoeist determines what craft fits best. When paddling a laundry tub on flat water, he discovers that no surge of superhuman effort will allow him to keep up with a sleek, narrow hull that vanishes around the next bend in seconds. Or he may be desperately banging down a boulder-decked rapids when a keelless, high-rockered white-water craft shoots past, the paddlers sideslipping their canoe effortlessly. Or he could be drowning in sweat on a steep portage trail, a heavy-hulled replica of the U.S.S. Enterprise forcing his collarbones down to his navel, when some 110-pound sprite of a girl comes whistling past, packsack on her back and canoe riding her shoulder pads like a feather.

If he has any intelligence at all, our struggling hero will, if possible, stop these varied folk for a moment and ask them about their craft. There is little that canoe folk like to do more than talk about their canoes, especially when it is obvious they are outperforming anything nearby.

Professional guides may or may not be a good source of information on canoes. Guides in some areas are quite knowledgeable about designs suited for their particular purposes, but some guides are in a mental straitjacket and would rather fight than switch.

Canoe clubs are a good source of information, if for no other reason than that the members usually have a great variety of craft. Almost any store selling canoe equipment will have the address of any such club nearby and is likely to have the name of the person to contact about meetings. There are several periodicals that cover canoeing, one of the best being *Canoe* magazine, incorporating the *Canoe/Kayak Buyer's Guide*, published by New England Publications, Inc., Highland Mill, Camden, Me. 04843. This highly specialized publication is written and edited by some of the most knowledgeable canoe people in North America.

Before buying a canoe, the prospective buyer may gain some idea by renting various craft from liveries. Paddling hulls of as many different types and sizes as possible will provide a lot of firsthand knowledge that you can't get by reading the manufacturer's literature. Remember, though, that empty canoes, particularly the shorter models, do not perform the same as canoes loaded with camping gear. The addition of a hundred pounds to the normal weight of two paddlers, or the addition of a third passenger, will usually give a clearer indication of what the canoe will do under actual cruising conditions. When a canoe performs well, or even if it doesn't, turn it upside down and sight down the keel line. That four to six inches of hull depth that was in the water determined what the canoe was doing. This is how to judge a hull, not by the gunwale trim or paint job.

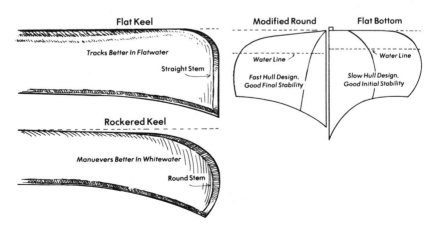

Flat-water or "lake" canoes very often have fin keels that stick down an inch or more. Ninety-nine canoe salesmen out of a hundred will insist that a keel is necessary to "make the canoe go straight." This is not exactly the truth. Most fin keels are structural members, particularly on aluminum canoes, holding the craft together and maintaining its shape. They have some limited value in helping canoes track straight in a wind, particularly if there is considerable rocker at the bow and stern. But a keel-free canoe with a good "V" entry and a straight line from bow to stern will hold a course with far less effort. If a keel was a necessity for lake travel, the voyageurs would never have gotten the first trade cargo from Montreal to Grand Portage.

Keels also serve as underwater "bumpers," to some extent protecting the hull from damage when rammed over boulders or logs. But that projecting keel may be somewhat less than desirable in certain types of white water where it can hang up on boulders or ledges and lead to a thorough dunking.

And since the type of water in which a canoe will be used may influence a decision on size and design, another consideration is what the canoe will be used for and who will be in it. Take a couple of lake travelers who wish to cover the country fast and maybe do a little racing on weekends: they might consider the sharp-nosed, narrow, high-performance rounded hulls in 17 to 18½ feet put out by Jensen, Sawyer, Mad River, Moore, and Dave Hazen. At the other extreme is the puddle fisherman, the guy who uses his craft to poke into remote lakes and beaver ponds and may do a little solo cruising. Extreme lightness, stability, and a short hull for brush breaking may sway him toward a featherweight 13- or 14-footer like the Grumman, Black River Packer, Mad River Compatriot, Old Town Carleton Pack, Voyageur Scout, or any of the fine hulls made by Barth Hauthaway.

A 15-footer can be used for occasional cruising by two people, offers good portability, and has more room for gear. Unfortunately the lines on some of these, particularly the blunt metal styles, tend to be what we call "floomp" canoes. That is, when paddlers attempt to put on a little steam, they lurch ahead, going "floomp . . . floomp . . . floomp" over the water.

Most flat-water travelers, unless they can afford several hulls (or even if they can't afford them, like many of us) will be looking for something with good speed, fair initial stability, good seaworthiness in a stiff wind, reasonable maneuverability in white water, and light enough weight to portage easily.

Generally, we are talking about a hull 16 to 18½ feet long, 32 to 36 inches across the beam, and 12 inches or more in depth amidships. Bow height will be moderate, keel line straight or with slight bow rocker, "V" entry and exit, moderate tumblehome or definite flare, and a rounded hull. Flat-bottom hulls "feel" safe in still water, draw less in shallows, but are not nearly as stable as a rounded hull in rough water and are distinctly slower. At one time or another, Lil and I have owned every flat-bottom Grumman model, lightweight and standard, from 13 to 18 feet. Currently we have 17 and 18 lightweights for fishing and hunting because they have good initial stability, but they are slower than rounder bottoms on a long cruise.

Alumacraft is lately doing some things to improve performance—rounding the bottoms and sharpening the ends on their Quetico CL models. The 18½-footer, at 71 pounds, probably is the best-performing aluminum hull around. As competition with molded hulls continues, there is every reason to believe that aluminum lines will get sharper and faster.

Fiberglass, Royalex, Oltonar, Kevlar, and other plastic lay-ups, as well as fiberglassed cedar strips, are creating their own revolution in the market. The plastics are extremely tough, form into superb lines (when the mold was made by a superb designer), and are light on the yoke. Our 18-foot Kevlar-skin Jensen flat-out flies over the water, and at 50 pounds is easily portaged in combination with a full pack. Four decades ago we bushed in with an 18-foot canvas hull that varied from 85 to 95 pounds, depending on moisture content. Today, I am not enthusiastic about anything over 75 pounds on the pads.

Since there are so many makers of plastic canoes, it pays to check dimensions, weight, and lay-up carefully. For sheer lightness, fiberglassed cedar strips are hard to top. We have paddled a couple of 18-footers that weighed under 35 pounds, but these were racers, not cruising models. Cedar strips can be made in the basement at home if the canoeist has some time and fair skill with tools.

The United States Canoe Association puts out an excellent strip-building manual by Charles Moore for $2.50 and full-sized working drawings for a Lynn Tuttle, USCA 18½-foot cruiser for

$1.50, through USCA treasurer Jim Mack, 606 Ross Street, Middlton, Ohio 45042. This association sets standards for canoe racing and also promotes races, cruises, and training sessions. The American Canoe Association, 4260 East Evans Avenue, Denver, Colorado 80222 is the governing body on Olympic competition.

River trippers, people who will be traveling more in currents than lakes, may well consider a keelless or shoe-keel canoe. It should have sufficient rocker fore and aft for quick turning and a rounded enough bottom to slide laterally. The seat arrangement should allow for quick kneeling without ribs or other appurtenances to pop your kneecap, and nothing to grab your feet if the time comes to abandon ship. Pads, of course, can be used to protect your knees from hazards. If the canoeist learned his trade in the East or Midwest where poling is standard on shallow streams, consideration will be given to sufficient beam for the standing stick pusher.

Aluminum will take one heck of a pasting and can still be hammered back out, but it also tends to grab and hang on to rocks and ledges. So-called standard weights are better than light-weights for stream work simply because the skin is thicker. If noise insults the paddler's ear drums, aluminum may not be his bag. Canoe designer Ralph Sawyer, now in the paddle business in Oregon, used to call metal craft "boom-a-looms." And indeed they are. But they are tough.

Royalex and Oltonar "sandwich" designs will dent but return to their original shape with a little time, applied heat, or both. Developments in these materials are coming so fast it is nearly impossible to keep up, but there are some real changes taking place, all to the advantage of the downriver rider. Some white-water buffs still prefer wood and canvas. Chestnuts or Old Towns will take a lot more abuse than most people think, and they'll slide over most obstacles. But the cost of a new wood-and-canvas canoe can give the average canoeist a few second thoughts before he commits his work of art to the grinning maw of a boulder-toothed chute.

An important consideration in any cruising canoe design is provision for equipping with a portage yoke. Some canoes, such as Alumacraft, come with an excellent built-in yoke. It can be bought separate and will fit many other canoes. We have also built serviceable, comfortable yokes out of oak, making our own pads.

Homemade Oak Yoke

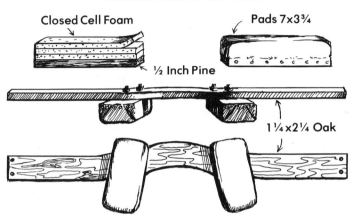

Closed Cell Foam

Pads 7x3¾

½ Inch Pine

1¼ x 2¼ Oak

There are, even at this late date, canoeists and canoe salespeople who pooh-pooh padded yokes, noting that "you can make a good yoke by lashing two paddles between the middle and front thwarts." Sure you can. To this statement, I always ask, "Oh, will you show me how it works?" One way or another, this usually provides a modicum of humor, if not when he tries to lash the paddles, then a moment later when he tries to roll the canoe and get his ears between the blades—and more entertainment when he tries to get it off. In order to keep the center thwart from wearing a notch in the cervical vertebrae and the blades from pulverizing the trapezius muscles, it is necessary to pad such a rig with jackets, sweaters, or a life vest—exactly why the yoke and pads came into existence in the first place. Furthermore, if you take a header with a yoked canoe, you can flip it free. If you fall while using a paddle rack, you're likely to be guillotined.

Another sales pitch to avoid is that "the high bow makes the canoe ride over the waves better." It doesn't. A canoe's seaworthiness in waves is determined by flare, tumblehome, and the height of the sides, not the height of the stem piece.

To sum up, the foregoing opinions may provide a few guidelines to the potential canoe purchaser, but they're not ironclad. Only after talking with other canoeists, looking at, poking at, sitting in, sighting down, paddling, and lifting a variety of canoes can you make a reasonable assessment.

At the same time, a peek at the price ticket may be a worthwhile exercise. Pricewise, a used canoe may be appealing. As with used cars, there are good used canoes and then there is what we call the Le Mon—which is plain old L-e-m-o-n. First, flip the canoe over and sight down the keel line to see if it is fairly straight, not too concave or too convex, and not twisted right or left. If it is aluminum, check for patched cuts. They're no problem if they're small, except along the keel, which could spell big trouble. Check the bow for replacement "shoes," which means that the original stem piece wore through and was covered over. Look for kinks where the hull may have been straightened, but not quite.

Check wood-and-canvas canoes for sound ribs, planking, and stem pieces and patches that may denote only a rip or maybe a piece of the hull torn out. Check the skin for cracks or looseness that may necessitate a new canvas job.

Fiberglass can be repaired so that damage is not easy to detect (and it may not even be a problem). But large areas that do not seem original may mean that the craft was in a major pileup. A close inspection of the gunwales may indicate where they were spliced when the sides were caved in. Worn spots on the outside of the hull will show matting through the gel coat.

Try out a used canoe before plunking down the coin. Not only put it in the water but also put water inside it. Blocked up on a couple of sawhorses or logs, a canoe partially filled with water will very quickly reveal where any leaks are. Know canoe prices. Retail markup on new canoes is about one-third. It is a little silly to pay more than two-thirds retail price for any used canoe unless it is in mint condition.

On the other hand, a good canoe, new or used, well taken care of, is a good investment. A new canoe depreciates a lot less—relatively speaking—than a new car. Also, as any water-oriented kid knows, there are very few really bad canoes. Even the most poorly designed, heavy, battered, patched, and splinted old relic—as long as it's watertight and sturdy—is better than no canoe at all.

Chapter 3

Paddle Skills

There are as many opinions about length, width, weight, materials, and shapes of canoe paddles as there are paddlers. Certainly centuries ago, native North American bark-canoe builders who created and tested the variations in canoe design—rockered, "V" bottom, hogged, straight keel, round nose, ram stem—were similarly involved in carving and testing a diversity of paddle styles. The evolution of paddle form is lost in antiquity, gone up in the smoke of ancient council fires where craftsmen compared and argued the relative merits of their carved creations.

From the evidence remaining, it is apparent that they developed countless styles from one-handed, ping-pong paddle types that were used by stalking hunters hunched below the gunwales, to sharp, narrow, six-foot models preferred for team effort on big water. Some paddles of ancient origin sported the "modern" T-grip. Others had no top grip at all, the paddler holding the shaft with his upper hand reversed, thumb down.

Today's recreational canoeist runs into a similar bewildering array of styles with the addition of a greater variety of materials.

One of the most frequent questions asked any outfitter is, "What kind of a paddle should I use?" To which most outfitters weasel an answer, "The one you paddle the best with."

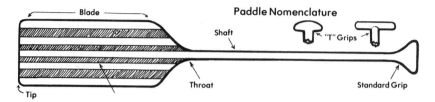

Not only is the confusion in paddles proliferated by the multitude of lengths, widths, and shapes, but there is a lot of disagreement among paddlers themselves over what constitutes a "good" paddle. Length is a particular area of controversy. A lot of books and pamphlets advocate (with appropriate illustrations) the selection of a paddle that reaches from the ground to the chin, nose, armpit, eyebrow—you name it. So many paddle myths have been created that the people who sell paddles are more apt to go along with the customers rather than get involved in a heated debate.

As an outfitter, with 200 paddles on the rack, I found that most men tended to select big paddles and most women picked smaller ones. The longest paddles I had were six feet, but I am sure that if I had seven-footers, some burly characters would have latched onto them simply because they were the longest available. The formula seemed to be: Big Man plus Big Paddle plus Big Strokes equals Big Speed. A plausible theory until a person witnesses his first canoe race and sees two Short Guys with Short Paddles using Short Strokes simply wipe the big guys off the map.

A paddle has its greatest efficiency when it is most nearly vertical in the water, all of the blade submerged. That is why the current top racers and cruisers use a relatively short, sharp stroke rather than the long sweep that was in vogue when I was a youngster. You can test this idea yourself. Take a long paddle and make a long stroke, starting at an angle way out in front, and ending up astern. You will note that when the paddle hits the water forward, some of the thrust is directed downward, in effect, lifting the canoe slightly. As the stroke comes back toward your knees, there is a distinct feeling of forward power. As the paddle trails off the stern, the effort is pulling the stern downward. Nearly half the stroke is wasted up and down, not forward.

Now try a shorter paddle. Start the stroke closer to your knees, make it abrupt, and bring it up before the blade gets much astern. Feels choppy, right? But see what the canoe is doing. A series of short strokes moves the canoe faster with less energy than those long sweeps. In racing, a jump from 54 to 60 strokes or more per minute can mean win instead of lose. The cruising canoeist is under no such pressure (unless a storm is brewing), but he can learn from the racers how to operate more efficiently, get more miles per gallon of sweat, and reach camp with fewer kinks in his arms and back.

Across North America, one of the great cruising and racing paddlers of this era is Gene Jensen of Minneapolis. Gene graciously consented to provide an analysis of a good cruising stroke. Here is how he describes it:

> The most important thing to remember is that you are propelling the canoe and not the paddle. Like any other physical exercise, the best result comes when the paddler can put as much of his or her total body strength into the task at hand. The more muscles one can use, the greater the total power output. At the same time, the elbows should flex as little as possible, as they act like a spring in absorbing the energy being transferred to the paddle.
>
> The paddler should be comfortably seated and with a foot brace, if possible. The brace should be approximately the length of the inseam in your slacks, from the front of the seat. A foot brace for the bowman is not as essential since the narrow foot space and the sharp angle of the sides allow the bowman to use this as a brace of sorts. Canoe manufacturers put the flotation in the ends, and the bulkhead can be used as a foot brace.
>
> Some paddlers like to put both feet out in front, while others like to put one out and one under the seat, switching them as they change paddling sides. This aids somewhat the rotating of the upper body during the stroke. Some paddlers put both legs under the seat in somewhat of a kneeling position. This tends to get your center of gravity down lower and make the canoe feel a little more stable, but it isn't the most comfortable position. . . . I have always had circulation problems in my feet and legs when trying the full kneel. I feel the most efficient way is to put both legs out in front

unless you are in a very narrow front seat or the space available just won't allow it.

The paddling techniques used by the best racers all seem to be a little different, but here are some general suggestions: Sit as erect as is comfortable; Hold the paddle with your hands spread apart about 24 to 28 inches. Reach forward, rotating the upper body and shoulders slightly toward the side the stroke will be on. Cock both arms slightly and keep them in that position throughout the stroke and return. Start the stroke driving both arms in a downward motion, at the same time rotating the shoulders and upper body in the direction of the stroke. Some of the paddlers bend a little from the waist during the stroke. This will tend to make the weight shift back and forth, causing the canoe to bob slightly. Sometimes, however, depending on the individual, the added punch will offset the bob and it helps rather than hurts the efficiency.

On the return of the stroke, I recommend rotating the paddle blade so that it is parallel with the water, holding the arms with the same bend as was used during the stroke, while rotating the body for the next stroke.

There, in a capsule, is what paddling is all about. Note the one distinct measurement: "hands spread apart 24 to 28 inches." Ah hah. When we are sitting down in paddling position, at mid-stroke the knuckles of the upper hand will be about eye level and the lower hand will be on the paddle throat, not halfway up the shaft. Why the throat? It is simply a matter of power. Anyone can test this by starting out with the lower hand gripping the throat. After a couple of strokes, move the lower hand up six inches and it becomes apparent that there is less thrust. Move the lower hand halfway up the shaft and you have difficulty paddling at all. In the correct position, to keep from rapping the lower knuckles on the gunwale, the shoulders are leaned out slightly over the blade.

O.K., so we measure the paddle by the shaft length, 24 to 28 inches between hands, depending on the person. The paddle blade can be any length, since it is in the water and has nothing to do with the hand position. A blade may be long, narrow, round, square, short, or squat, depending on what it is being used for. But once a paddler learns what his most efficient shaft length is, he can adapt that measurement to any shape of blade.

With paddle length settled, the next consideration is material and style. Solid wood paddles have been around for several thousand years and are still popular. Spruce, ash, and maple are favored in commercial blades, although other woods, including pine, work well. The current problem with solid wood paddles is in locating planks with straight grain. To get a paddle "worked down" into shape, some strength must be sacrificed. Solid wood paddles usually run about 6¾ inches to 7 inches wide. Anything wider invites a split where the edges get progressively weaker.

Quality laminated paddles maintain their strength through alternate straight-grain strips and tough bonding adhesives. Thus, wider, stronger paddles are possible at the same time offering thinner, lighter blades. Good laminated paddles have considerable springiness, allowing for some extra-heavy pressure when needed and also exerting a cushioning effect on the shoulders. We make our own pine/cedar laminated paddles, using 7 laminations in the shaft, 9 in the blade.

Theory Of The Hooked Paddle

Each paddle is 57 inches overall, has an eight-inch-wide blade, and is 34 inches from the top of the grip to the throat. Our hands are 27 inches apart while paddling. The paddle tip is slotted with an ash kerf, across grain for strength. Total weight of each paddle is under two pounds.

These are "hooked" paddles with a curve at the throat so that the blade is more nearly vertical at the point of greatest power. Also, they are slightly bent and deeply grooved at the base of the grip to fit our individual hands. This is an aid in sliding the upper hand in position quickly when we switch sides. These paddles are fitted to our own idiosyncrasies developed over 29 years of paddling together. We also have a number of straight paddles and a few plastic ones. The hooked paddle is a powerful cruising blade but does some weird things in white water. On river trips we prefer straight paddles.

Some fine commercial wood paddles are made by Sawyer, Clement, Cadorette, Chestnut, Old Town, and Shaw-Tenney. There are also some very low-priced, bargain-basement sticks available that can barely wait to get in the water so they can crack, split, or snap off.

There are some very, very nice asymmetrical paddles made by people like Azzali, who cater to the white-water racing trade, but they ain't cheap. If I ever owned one, I would probably have it chained to my wrist. Seda has some fine racing blades in spruce, mahogany, and maple.

Tough fiberglass and plastic paddles are gaining in popularity, particularly among river runners where paddle damage is a continual threat, and also among canoe rental operators who find their clients using paddles for poling, prying rocks, and (it is suspected) chopping wood. Fiberglass can be frayed or "chewed" with use but is easily repaired. Plastic such as ABS does not damage easily on the edges. Composition blades come with wood or aluminum shafts. The better aluminum shafts are foam-filled and coated so the hands won't turn black from the metal, or purple from cold.

Some good models are Iliad, Inc., T-grip, oval shaft; Krueger, 10-inch blade and 23-ounce weight; Seda, with both polyester and epoxy-Kevlar; Harmony Paddles, T-grip, coated oval shaft, molded epoxy blade, metal impact plate that rates very high for whitewater; and Bart Hauthaway with fir-shafted fiberglass paddles, including specialized model for one-man canoes. In the ordinary family paddle range, Carlisle ABS blades with aluminum shafts are serviceable and inexpensive; Mohawk and

Duralux have some tough plastic blades in the same price range.

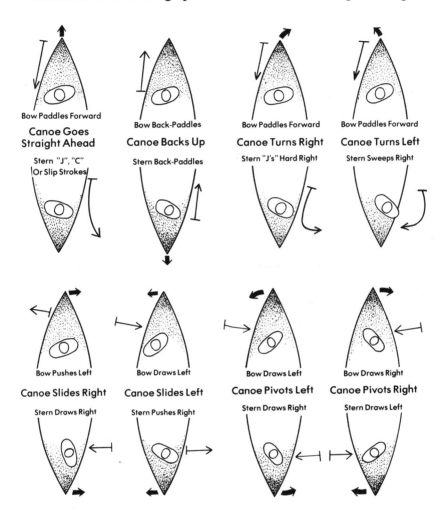

To control the canoe, paddlers should know how to make it go straight, right, left, back up, move sideways, and turn around on its axis. Only a few basic strokes are required.

Let's say we have our canoe sitting on the water with no wind, bowman paddling on the left side, stern man on the right. Both paddlers make straight strokes, pulling the canoe ahead. But not only does it move ahead; it also moves slightly left. At canoe liveries this is known as the "homing instinct." It is a phenomenon of novice paddlers who discover to their amazement that the canoe tends to make a big circle right back to the dock. The reason is the difference in location of the two paddles in relation to the canoe.

If a canoe had two slots in the bottom so that both paddles came straight back on the keel line, the canoe would move straight ahead. But, in practice, the bowman is inserting his blade up toward the stem and pulling it back about 12 inches left of the keel line. The stern man is inserting his blade about midway between bow and stern and is pulling it back some 16 inches to the right of the keel. This lopsided effect is what makes the canoe keep veering to the left.

To compensate, some beginners use the stern paddle as a rudder, angling it out the back to bring the bow back on course. But this practice causes a loss in forward power. In a headwind, the canoe may simply stop.

Next is the "J-stroke," which is accomplished by turning the knuckles of the lower hand toward the canoe at the end of the stroke and pushing the blade outward. A slight "J" will make the canoe turn to the right. To go left, the "J" is abandoned and the paddle brought back in a sweeping outward curve toward the stern, in effect "drawing" the stern to the right, making the bow go left.

Unlike steering a car, where the front wheels turn and the back wheels pivot to follow the front, here we have the bow making the pivot, the stern moving to the right or left to change direction.

Experienced paddlers usually discover that they can get the same effect of a J-stroke by just angling the paddle blade slightly from the middle of the stroke back without pushing out to the side. This is sometimes called a "slip stroke."

I just mentioned the term "drawing." This, coupled with "prying" and "pushing," makes one end or both ends of the canoe go directly sideways. A "draw" is made simply by reaching out to the side and pulling the flat blade of the paddle back to the canoe. If it is done at opposite ends simultaneously, the canoe will pivot on its axis.

A "pry" is made by placing the blade below the hull, the shaft touching the side, both hands up high to clear the gunwale and the shaft pulled inward with a levering motion, the gunwale being the fulcrum. Some people are very fast with this maneuver, but there is a tendency for the gunwale to chew away at the paddle shaft, and there is also the possibility of the blade's jamming between two rocks, which could snap the paddle or lever the paddler right into the drink. I think it's easier to maintain the hands in the regular position and just push the paddle away from the hull—the opposite of the draw. When this pushing motion is used lengthwise with the canoe, it causes the canoe to back up and is called a "back stroke."

There is another important paddle position, not exactly a stroke, which is called the "brace." It starts out the same as the draw except the paddle isn't pulled back to the canoe. Instead, the paddler leans out and holds the paddle flat. The brace is used to increase stability in wind, waves, white water, launching, beaching, and when your partner socks into a six-pound bass and goes bananas.

There is a "cross brace" and "cross draw," which means that if you were paddling on the right side, you would swing the paddle over to the left without changing your hand position, just your arms and shoulders completing the movement. White-water racers are good at this, but I am a switch paddler and prefer to change hands when I change sides.

A few moments ago I noted that short, quick strokes move a canoe faster and with less effort than long strokes. Racers (and increasingly more cruisers) have discovered that changing sides every few strokes reduces fatigue by resting one set of muscles and putting another in play. But doesn't this constant switching result in less speed? No sirree. With a little practice that switch can be done without a break in stride. Racers switch on every five, ten, or so strokes with the stern man calling "hut!" or some agreed signal on a downstroke. The switch is made as the blade is being brought forward. The lower hand slides up from the throat, and as it reaches the middle of the shaft, the upper hand releases the grip and drops to the throat. The other hand continues up to the grip as the paddle moves over the canoe and down the other side, starting the next stroke. Not only is this less tiring, but by putting more strokes on one side than the other, the stern paddler can compensate for a strong side-wind without wasting much effort J-stroking.

When cruising, Lil and I do not operate as hyper as the racers, but usually we change sides about every 20 strokes. We sometimes sing or hum along in rhythm, with the words "18 ... 19 ... 20" signaling the switch. Racers punch along at 54 to 70 strokes per minute. Lil and I swing 30 to 45 strokes per minute on a cruise and can hit the pump in a spurt of 60 or so if we need it.

Most paddlers develop a preference for either bow or stern, and most paddle stronger on one side than the other, although this is not as apparent with teams that continually switch. Less-experienced paddlers tend to think the stern paddler is more "important" than the bowman. In flat water, their contribution is equal. In white water, the bowman might be considered the more "important"—if there is such a thing.

The value of a good bowman becomes painfully apparent when a camper takes a solo cruise. Simple arithmetic would indicate that one paddler would travel half as fast as two. He doesn't. He is lucky if he can go a third as fast. With the usual wind problems (in your face going out, in your face coming back) the loner has his work cut out for him. In an empty canoe, a single paddler will usually operate best by sitting in the bow seat, facing backward toward the stern. Or he can put a big rock in the bow. With a load forward he can paddle from the stern, but in wind he'll probably go best by getting on his knees somewhere just back of the center thwart.

There is some freedom cruising alone, going where you want without consultation. I have taken solo trips of 250 miles or so but found that talking to seagulls and turtles is less than stimulating. Luckily for me, I have had the same bow paddler for 29 years. She pushes a good paddle, swings a mean fish rod, and is a pleasant all-weather camper. You find one like that, buddy, you hang on.

Three paddlers can shove a canoe along at a good clip if the third paddler sits on a pack between the center and bow thwarts. To balance up, all of the other packs are stowed between the center thwart and the stern paddler. We cruise at about 20 strokes and then switch, but with a couple of differences. The bow and stern paddlers both paddle on the same side, the middle paddler on the odd side. Believe it or not, the canoe will track straight. To miss the bowman on the switch, the middle paddler may lose a count and may have to shift slightly on the seat to reach over the gunwale, but it usually takes only a little practice to pick up the three-man beat.

All canoeists develop their own likes in paddles and begin to doodle ideas of their own. Anyone with fair skill can carve out a paddle if he can find a piece of straight-grained wood. We make laminated paddles out of eight sawn, 24-inch-long strips each planed to 13/16-inch square for the blade, seven 1½-inch-wide by 58-inch strips each planed 3/16-inch thick for the shaft and four blocks 1½ x 11/16 x 3 inches for the grip. The thin shaft strips are glued, then clamped and dried. The grip and blade strips are glued, clamped to the shaft, and dried. Removed, the rough paddle is trimmed for length, a one-inch groove is sawed at the foot of the blade, and an ash kerf strip is glued in place. When this is dry, the blade, shaft, and grip are worked down, care being taken to remove material equally from both sides of the blade. Sanded and varnished with three coats, it's ready to go. We paint distinct, identifying designs on each blade with machinery en-amel. These are *our* paddles, and there ain't no others like them in the world.

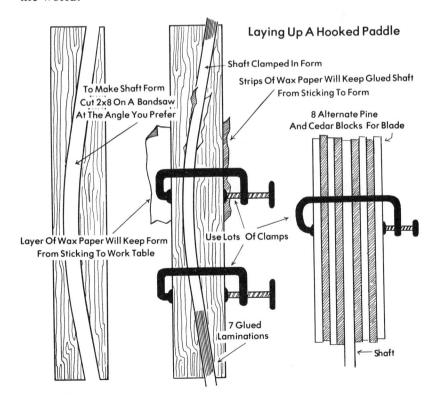

Laying Up A Hooked Paddle

Shaft Clamped In Form

Strips Of Wax Paper Will Keep Glued Shaft From Sticking To Form

To Make Shaft Form Cut 2x8 On A Bandsaw At The Angle You Prefer

8 Alternate Pine And Cedar Blocks For Blade

Layer Of Wax Paper Will Keep Form From Sticking To Work Table

Use Lots Of Clamps

7 Glued Laminations

Shaft

Chapter 4

Packing and Portaging

The word "portage" derives from the French word "porter," which means to carry. As a noun, portage describes a trail between two water areas; as a verb portage is what happens when a canoe runs out of navigable water and must be packed overland with the gear. On a short haul with a light load, a portage is a welcome respite from paddling. On a long trail with a heavy load and maybe a mosquito-laden drizzle thrown in, it tends to test the will as well as the vocabulary.

Ideally, the canoe and equipment should balance out so that two paddlers make every portage in one trip. In simple math, two paddlers making a mile portage in one trip walk one mile each. If they have to go back for more gear, they walk a mile back and another mile over again for a total of three miles. A double portage isn't double; it's triple.

Much of the extended portaging and multiple trips seen on north country trails is the result of some rather bizarre methods of packing. From time to time, you see cardboard boxes, laundry bags, plastic sacks, wooden crates, foam coolers, and various other containers stuffed to the brim with equipment and foodstuffs, all being portaged—and not very successfully. Centuries ago, nomadic humans found it much easier to transport loads in a single bag on their backs rather than in hand-held bundles. The packsack has been improved on but not yet replaced.

The Duluth pack, essentially a big canvas bag with shoulder straps, is the standard carryall over much of the north. The #3 Duluth, 28 inches by 30 inches with a double canvas bottom, heavy-duty flap, and adjustable leather shoulder harness, is most commonly used. For freighting, it is sometimes rigged with a tumpline (head strap), but this accessory is ordinarily not required with today's lightweight gear. The best thing about Duluth packs is that they fit nicely inside a canoe, since they were specifically designed for this use. Two packs will fit side by side between the gunwales. Four can be fitted, two on either side of the center thwart. Six (heaven forbid) can be carried in one canoe in a pinch.

But Duluth packs have a few drawbacks: they ride low on your back, pull badly on your shoulders, and do not protect your back from hard objects inside. Unless padded, a metal item like a cook kit will bore a hole right into your spinal column. However, handled correctly, the Duluth packs do a creditable job.

Two men on a trip of up to two weeks can make it with all the equipment in one Duluth pack, all the food in another. When we portage, the partner who carries the canoe also carries the gear pack. His companion takes the heavier food pack plus any odds and ends such as fishing tackle. If the canoe is extra heavy, we settle that as one load, the other person taking both Duluth packs, one balanced above the other, just behind the head. On longer trips with two food packs, the canoe carrier doubles with canoe and pack, his partner takes two packs. This system isn't recommended for newcomers, but it can be worked into after a few days on the trail.

Big loads can be carried more easily with form-fitting aluminum pack frames, nylon bags, and padded harnesses that put the loads high on the shoulders. Furthermore, these packs have compartments that make it easier to locate critical items such as the map, first-aid kit, or toilet paper. But they have their drawbacks, too. Most pack frames are awkward to load and unload from a canoe. Worse, most of them project above the shoulders, making it difficult or impossible to carry a pack and portage a canoe at the same time.

A few pack frames are built short enough to get under a canoe yoke. Camp Trails makes a good one, and this is the type we use. They hang a little lower and are not as comfortable for extended backpacking, but they work O.K. on a canoe trip. These come with a deep sack and no open frame space to tie on a sleeping bag. On some trips we use a combination of bags—the equipment in a Duluth pack, the food in the pack frame. The equipment bag, with both sleeping bags, has a heavy-duty plastic liner sealing the entire interior from water. Since we pack our food in individual plastic bag meal units, a liner is not necessary in the frame pack, though we sometimes use one.

When Lil and I go, we split the portage load so I have the canoe (50 to 75 pounds) plus the gear (25 pounds) and Lil has the food (50 pounds) plus a few pounds of PFDs (personal flotation devices), cameras, and fishing gear. And that's it. As the trip goes on, the food pack gets smaller and we move some of the items not affected by water, such as the cook kit, tent stakes, etc., over from my pack to balance out. We usually wind up with all the food gone, all the gear plus the extra pack stowed in the food pack, and all I am toting is the canoe.

Obviously, we don't haul "extras." We have seen canoeists with hip boots, folding chairs, gas lanterns, radios, portable tape decks, you name it. If they want to haul it, that's their party. But there isn't a whole lot of stuff a canoeist really *needs*.

For ordinary summer trips, here is the gear Lil and I pack: canoe, three paddles, two packsacks, two PFDs, tent and fly, poles and pegs, kitchen fly, two synthetic fiber sleeping bags, two foam mats, rope, repair kit, first-aid kit, cook kit and utensils, folding saw, dish-washing gear, toilet kit and towel, map and compass, flashlight, candles to read by and a couple of paperback books, pencil and pad, camera and films, bug repellant, aerosol bomb, and fishing tackle.

We have personal items such as knife and matches, wristwatch, a coil of ⅛-inch nylon line, and a bandana. Lil wears sunglasses. Other than the clothes on our backs, we carry rain suits and one extra pair of sox each. We wash sox and underwear every other day, shirts and pants when they get unbearable. We haven't gotten down to using the same toothbrush to save weight, but we have talked about it.

To load the gear into the Duluth pack, we first insert the liner.

Making Up A Duluth Gear Pack

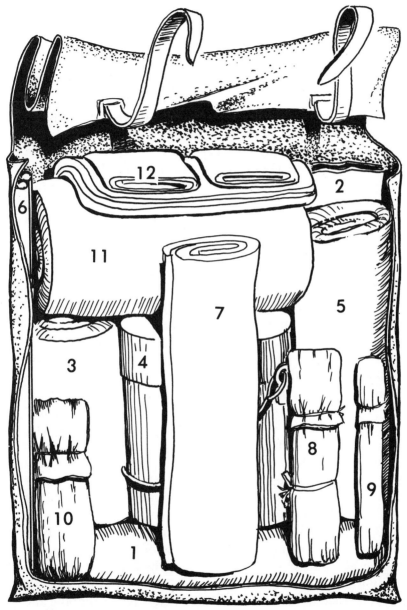

1. Foam Mat 2. Kitchen Fly 3. Tent 4. Cook Kit 5. Sleeping Bag
6. Tent Poles 7. Foam Mat 8. Utensils 9. Saw 10. Pegs
11. Sleeping Bag 12. Rain Gear

On the bottom goes one foam mat. On this, upright, against one side goes the tent (with fly rolled up inside). On the other side goes a sleeping bag, the cook kit in the middle. The kitchen tarp goes between the cook kit and the back of the bag (padding), the second foam mat goes down the front, and the last sleeping bag on top. Then we hold the sides of the Duluth pack and firm this all down with one knee. Tent poles, stakes, saw, and extra sox are stuffed down the sides. The plastic liner is closed. Rain gear is laid directly under the flap and the pack buckled down, then laid on a flat surface, backstraps down, and smoothed out with hands and knees to make a nice, square package.

If we are using two Duluth packs, we make up the food pack with a plastic liner and reinforce it with a cardboard box inside (some coffee cartons such as Arco fit perfectly). The box keeps the food from being damaged. As the end of the trip nears, the box may be burned.

In the early spring or on fall hunting trips, our one-pack-per-person rule gets bent pretty far, since extra food, clothing, bigger sleeping bags, and so on all add bulk and weight. But on most summer trips we have one pack each and travel quite comfortably. And we save a lot of time on portages.

Most people have little difficulty with packsacks, properly balanced and moderately loaded, but some people have difficulty with canoes. The initial problem is "flipping" a canoe up with a one-man lift. This is a lot easier to demonstrate than to describe in words. For several years, Harry Lambirth, Sandy Bridges, and I were instructors in state-certified guide schools in Duluth, Eveleth, and Ely, Minnesota, where we taught several hundred people—from 110-pound girls to college athletes—to portage canoes. Every student learned to roll up the craft. That's what it really amounts to: rolling it up. It is a method essentially the same as used by most of the guides we know and it works like this:

Standing at a point amidships, the canoeist grabs the near gunwale with both hands and pulls the canoe up on its side, the keel against his knees. Next, with the knees half bent, the canoe is pulled upward until it rests as far up on the lap as it will go. The right hand reaches out and grabs the center thwart, tipping the canoe upward, the left hand grasping the far gunwale just ahead of the center thwart. Now, with the canoe held solidly against the body by the left hand, legs still in a half crouch, the right hand slides off the thwart and goes underneath the near gunwale at the thwart, "cradling" that gunwale so it rests in the crook of the right arm. With one continual lifting movement of the right arm, and a simultaneous pulling across the head and down with the left arm, the craft is "rolled" to the shoulders, the yoke pads sliding in on either side of the neck. With the right hand still cradling the craft, the left hand slides forward to grip the gunwale at arm's length, and the right hand follows.

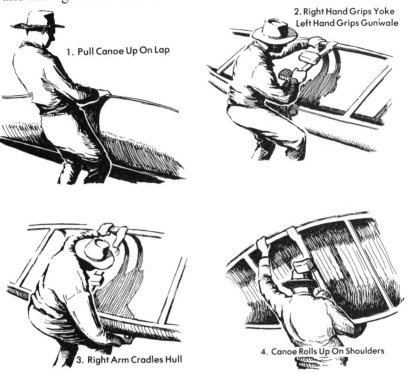

1. Pull Canoe Up On Lap

2. Right Hand Grips Yoke
Left Hand Grips Gunwale

3. Right Arm Cradles Hull

4. Canoe Rolls Up On Shoulders

To get the canoe down again, exactly the reverse course is followed. The left hand steadies the craft while the right arm slides around the gunwale in the cradling movement. The left hand slides back to the gunwale by the center thwart and lifts slightly so the head can slide out from between the yoke pads, the canoe continuing over and down gently, cradled on the right arm and to the bent knees, and then to the ground. In this method, the canoe is never dropped. It is always in balance. Neither the front nor the stern will bang against the ground. This method is also easiest on the arms, wrists, and neck.

It is, of course, no sin for two people to help each other up with the canoe if neither can flip it. With this method, the partners turn the canoe upside down and each grabs the near gunwale by the front seat. Then they raise the bow above their heads. One canoeist holds it up while the other crouches underneath and slips his shoulders into the yoke. Both canoeists cross the portage together, but only one carries the canoe. On the far side, the stern is lowered to the ground and one partner holds the bow up while his canoe-toting companion slides out from under the pads. Then together they lower the craft to the ground by the gunwales in front. Once in a while, a canoe does not balance out from the center thwart, but this problem can be solved by tying a life jacket under the seat of the light end.

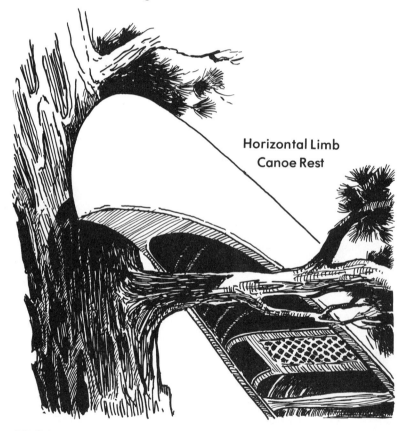

Horizontal Limb
Canoe Rest

Walking a canoe over the trail becomes old stuff with time. In our younger days, we used to grab up the craft and run the portage, packsack and all. Nowadays we're content with a steady walk. Until the packer gets accustomed to portaging the canoe, he should spend little time rubbering around at the scenery. A log, boulder, or stob can trip the unwary, putting him on his face with the canoe on top. An overhead branch, not observed in advance, can shove the canoe sideways and knock the packer off balance. Spring rains can make portages slick as a greased doorknob. Once, when crossing a semisubmerged trail near Ontario's Hematite Lake, I slid into a moose wallow, canoe on top, and spent a good ten minutes floundering out of the ooze while Lil nearly expired with laughter.

Usually, it pays to take a little time in portaging. And if the breath starts sticking near the sternum, stop for a moment. On some well-traveled routes there may be canoe "rests," poles spiked or lashed between two trees about eight feet above the ground. In remote areas, two trees growing almost together, a forked tree or a large, low, near-horizontal limb will suffice.

Eventually, the trail ends at the water again and the canoe is launched. It is at this point that considerable canoe damage may occur. The packer is tired. The canoe has doubled its weight on his shoulders. When he rolls the canoe off, it may slip and land with a bang. If a good, sharp rock is handy, it will obligingly ventilate the hull. Where possible, we walk to the shore and lower the canoe so the bow extends over the water. If the canoe does happen to get off balance, the bow hits water instead of rock.

Early explorers noted that native Indian canoemen sometimes waded into the water to put down their fragile birchbark craft. Some canoeists we know today, who put a high value on a finely handcrafted hull, do the same thing. A dented, scraped, patched hull does not necessarily indicate a veteran canoeman with years of experience.

So far I've talked about two canoeists packing across. When there are three to a canoe, loads can be balanced out between the canoe and the three or four packs involved—and the portage still made in one trip. It's when the party gets down to solo travel that the packing gets sticky. To keep weights within one man's packing ability, canoes can be scaled down to fifty pounds or less, along with a lighter shelter and a reduced food pack. Otherwise, double trips on the portages are unavoidable. I have bushed alone with a Grumman 15-foot lightweight (55 pounds), extra paddle, nylon tarp, mosquito net, bag, ground cloth, one cook pot and cup, utensils (spatula, spoon, fork, knife), toilet kit, food, and darn little else, and made every portage in one trip.

One last observation on portaging: Canoeists traveling the Canadian backcountry will occasionally run across a paddle leaning against a tree, traps cached on a platform, an old tea pail stashed under a rock, or a trail marker of some kind. In no instance should these items be removed and hauled away for souvenirs. It is a safe bet they belong to some Indian trapper who knows exactly where he left them and will expect to find them there the next time he comes through by canoe or on snowshoes. People who live in the woods often leave items along the trail just as suburbanites leave garden tools in the backyard leaning against the garage. Northern residents do not appreciate having their possessions moved any more than a city dweller would appreciate our Ojibwa or Cree neighbors coming down and removing his street sign, house number, or the tires off his car.

Chapter 5

How Canoes Tip People Over

Although I have carefully examined hundreds of canoes, I have never been able to locate a single muscle, tendon, blood vessel, or indication of a nervous system. But canoes must have these features because they "tip over" when people get in them, just about the way broncos buck riders off. During the years Lil and I outfitted wilderness trips, we had numerous soggy folk relate how, in a fit of perversity, the canoe deposited passengers and duffle in the water.

Oddly enough, no one has ever witnessed this phenomenon when a canoe was empty. An empty canoe sits docilely in the water, about like the way that mean bronco waits quietly in the chute before a rider gets aboard. But when packs, passengers, or both are added to canoes, they apparently plot treachery.

Now, Lil and I have never experienced this phenomenon. Every time we were involved with the canoe in some mishap, it was the result of what aviators call "P.E."—the abbreviation for Pilot Error. Either I dunnit, Lil dunnit, somebody with us dunnit, or we all dunnit. It was some sort of miscalculation that proved one trait all canoes have in common: they leak over the top. Whatever measures the canoeists can take to prevent this leakage makes the trip more pleasant.

The first possibility for trouble comes when the paddler, canoe, and water all meet for the first time: loading up. Where possible, the canoe should be in the water and broadside to the beach, rock shelf, or log landing. One canoeist steadies the craft by the gunwales while his companion places the packsacks between the gunwales, balancing the weight so that the craft will ride evenly from side to side and from front to back. If the canoe must be loaded while it's angling out from shore, the bowman climbs in, drops to his knees behind the center thwart, positions the packsacks one at a time as his partner hands them in, and then

Loading Canoe

slips into the bow seat. Where the shoreline is so shallow that the canoe will be grounded when loaded, we simply wade out in boots and socks and load it while standing in the water. Once the canoe is loaded and the bowman is in place, the stern paddler eases his end toward deeper water and then slides into his seat. Some canoeists launch with a great shove and a flying leap to one knee on the stern deck, a spectacular feat if the canoe doesn't smack a hidden rock or log. Over the long haul, it is drier to just step into the canoe, sit down, and push off with the paddle.

A couple of rules about getting in, getting out, and moving about inside a canoe are not subject to amendment: When stepping in, the canoeist leans over, grips the gunwales, and places his feet on the center line. Every time. When he gets out, he leans over, grips the gunwales, and, with one foot on the centerline, puts the other foot ashore. If footing is firm, he transfers his weight to the shore foot. If footing is not firm, he will not lose his balance nor unbalance the canoe while his weight is centered and his hands are on the gunwales. No one but a rank amateur will teeter in or out of a canoe with his hands full of gear.

While the first canoeist is getting out, his partner is holding the canoe steady with a paddle brace or with the blade anchored on the bottom.

Many a canoe is rolled over when the bow is rammed up on the shore while landing or when the canoe has been beached and the bowman leaps out and pulls his end up on higher ground, causing the craft to balance precariously between the stem and the narrow portion of the stern near the rear seat. Where shoreline conditions permit, the craft is beached sideways with draw or pry strokes. One man steps out and steadies the craft while the other steps out and then begins unloading duffle.

Where the craft must be beached bow-first, it is eased into the shallows, the bowman locates solid ground, steps out, and steadies the craft while the stern man slides over the duffle and out over the bow. For the hull's sake, it pays to come in slow in case the landing is decorated with sharp underwater rocks or maybe an old timber left over from logging days, festooned with iron spikes.

Once paddlers are aboard a canoe and underway, they always keep their rear ends centered on the seat. They can lean outward, move their arms, legs, and upper torso, but the tail end is always centered. Canoes fitted with bucket seats anchor the paddler in place. Webbed seats tend to acquire a little sag in time and prevent much tail movement, but a conscious effort to stay centered must be maintained.

Guides dread a day on the water with a "butt-shifter." In 1967, three days after ice-out, I was on Quetico Park's McAree Lake with a young man, fishing lake trout below Rebecca Falls. He turned out to be not only a butt-shifter but also a stand-upper, an unsettling turn of events with snow still on the ground and the water about 40 degrees. Hooking his first seven-pound trout, he slid from gunwale to gunwale, then stood up while I braced first right, then left, yelling for him to sit down. He dropped back in place, and I netted the fish. A moment later he hooked another trout, repeated his gyrations, and finally sat down while the second fish came to net. At this point I leaned forward, looked him straight in the eye and hissed, "You stand up once more or even wiggle your tail end off center on that seat, sonny, and I am going to take this paddle and tear your head clear off." We had a remarkably safe, quiet day thenceforth.

As noted before, the canoe load is usually trimmed level, both side to side and front to stern. However, any difference in weight between the bow and stern paddlers must be considered and the packs shifted accordingly. A bow-heavy canoe will not steer correctly on flat water, and a stern-heavy canoe is subject to wind shift. Where rough water lies ahead and the canoeists drop to their knees, the move will shift the weight slightly forward and this should be anticipated when possible. In white water, some paddlers prefer to have the bowman kneeling *behind* the bow seat to center his weight and give the bow more buoyancy. If this is the plan, then the packs must be arranged to allow him ample leg room and the shift must be made in slack water, not when the haystacks are looming up.

Even though he uses much skill and takes reasonable precautions, any canoeist who spends a lot of time on lakes and streams under a variety of conditions must anticipate getting dunked sometime. U.S. and Canadian law generally requires canoeists to carry personal floatation devices, known as PFDs. For canoe use, only those types that can be worn as a vest should be considered. Boat cushions and so-called ski belts are not worth much except at night as tent pillows.

PFDs are required by law to be U.S. Coast Guard approved. This means they have been tested for construction, materials, and ability to hold a person afloat. A true USCG "life jacket," one that will hold a person upright in the water even when unconscious, is the inflatable tube type found aboard seagoing vessels. These jackets are subject to leaks, require CO_2 cartridges for inflation, and are clumsy when paddling. To accommodate the recreational user, the Coast Guard has sanctioned "Class III" devices, which will float a person but may not hold him upright with his head out of the water. If a canoe swamps, it is important to immediately check everybody involved to see that they are conscious, uninjured, and swimming—not floating face down.

There are several lightweight Class III PFDs that allow good arm movement while you're paddling. In our area, the Stearns panel-type vest is in common use. It is large enough to go over summer clothing easily or snug enough to go under a hunting jacket. The Seda Whitewater vest is tube-constructed and hinged at the waist to allow for kneeling. Other good vests are Omega High Performance Sport Vest; Medalist "Cut and Jump"; A. B. Sea Model S, tube vest; America's Cup Pro-Classic 101, panel-type; Taperflex Model NCMG; and Gentex Guardian.

When you shop for a vest, try it on in the store. Carefully check the fit as well as all the zippers, ties, hooks, and other closures. It is good practice to buckle on the jacket, pick a paddle off the store rack, sit down on a chair or canoe seat, and try the device for comfort and freedom of movement, noting any tendency of closures, panels, tubes, or stitching to rub anywhere. Check the vest again in the kneeling position. A good PFD may cost as much as a good paddle but is cheap insurance when you consider that it should last ten years.

Anyone who has been involved in or has witnessed a few swampings will verify one fact about PFDs: they are extremely difficult to buckle on when a person is in the water—almost impossible when the vest is floating on the surface and the canoeist is on the bottom of the river. Poor swimmers should wear them all the time. Experienced canoeists who can swim sometimes paddle without jackets on calm water, but keep them within easy reach. Some people make a practice of tying their life jackets securely under their canoe seats—a shrewd move only if the canoe is worth more than the people. Better keep them handy.

Canoes usually swamp either in white water, the subject of Chapter 6, or in wind, which I'll talk about right here. In any group discussion of wind and waves, somebody usually says, "I'd rather be in a canoe in rough water than in a boat." A couple of things are amiss with this thesis, the first being that a canoe *is* a boat, the second that it ain't built for use in high seas, unless it happens to be a 34-foot Canot du Nord or something similar. The best designed recreational canoe, 16, 17, or 18 feet long, is no match in rough water for a well-designed dory the same length. The experienced canoeist who notes waves building up that his canoe may not handle simply doesn't get into them. The trick is in knowing what size those waves are, something usually learned after considerable trial and error, or trial and luck.

An otherwise-empty canoe, with the paddlers kneeling, can take two-foot, three-foot, or bigger waves if the paddlers are good. A loaded canoe will ride a little lower and handle more sluggishly. The best way to learn about waves is to put on swimming suits in the summertime, paddle a little distance offshore, and try the craft out in the wind. By quartering into the waves, hitting them nose-on, quartering away, or running downwind, paddlers can quickly pick up some rough-water seamanship. They will note that every fourth or fifth wave, the one that breaks right on the gunwale, is the one that will "getcha."

Heading straight into the waves will work in a chop, but in a heavy sea the bow will rise up over the crest and drop with a smash. Then the water will come in alongside the bow paddler's seat. It is better to quarter into the waves at an angle, riding up and across the face of each wave and across and down the back. Paddling is done in the trough, and a brace is applied at the crest to prevent rolling sideways. For instance, when the canoe is climbing a wave, the bow paddler is bracing on the crest (leaning out on his flattened paddle), the stern paddler still driving forward. As the canoe goes over the top and down toward the trough, the bow paddler is driving forward, the stern man bracing. This is usually only necessary on that fourth or fifth really big wave; on the smaller ones, both are paddling. If you keep a sharp eye out for breaking waves, the canoe can be speeded up or slowed down in the trough to avoid them.

Very often trouble occurs while you're running with the wind, especially coming off a lee shore where the canoeists are reading the backs of the big waves and from a distance. There are indications of rough water if the treetops are being whipped around and if there are flickers of white far up the lake where the water is slamming in against the shore. Once the canoe is committed downwind, there is no turning back without the danger of broaching and swamping. A downwind ride can be exhilarating, but tricky. Before getting into the "stuff," some canoeists load their craft a little bow-heavy to make the stern ride higher. We generally maintain the same trim, but we drop forward on our knees. Running with the waves, the canoe will pick up speed as it climbs the crest. Then it slows abruptly as it loses the crest and rides down the reverse face of the next wave. There is seldom any problem going "up" a wave. It is possible to get up enough speed to pick up a good comber and "surf" for some distance; but once forward speed is cut, the danger comes from the following wave breaking over the stern. Again, it is good procedure to try this out in an unloaded craft while wearing swim suits, long before any extended cruise on big lakes.

By studying the map and the terrain, you can chart a course across windswept waters to take advantage of islands and points. Wind acts much like running water in that it swirls behind obstructions, creating eddies. For instance, a headwind cutting around a point of land may have a strong reverse air current along shore that the canoeists can pick up and ride "upwind." Waves breaking across a point will often be sharper and meaner than out in the middle of the lake. So, when you enter such a sea from quiet water, it is well to attack at a long quartering angle, the bowman paddling in the upwind side, stern man on the lee side so the bow paddler can draw, if necessary to keep heading into the wind.

In any rough sea, some slop will come in. If your gear is sealed against water, it will stay dry. Prior to the advent of plastic pack liners, the old-timers put a few two-inch saplings on the canoe bottom, which created a "bilge" that allowed the packs to ride high and dry. A little slop is no problem, but if it builds up, particularly in a flat-bottom canoe, it can shift and cause capsizing. We often carry a boat sponge jammed up under a pack strap. Dry, it weighs nothing. But it is excellent for taking out excess water. In a big sea, we break out a cook pail for a bailer, tying it to the canoe with a three-foot leash so it won't vanish if dropped accidently overside. Some canoeists use an empty plastic bleach jug, cut in half on a bevel.

In any confrontation with big water and rough water, it is essential that the gear be lashed to the canoe. When a canoe swamps, it fills to the gunwales and becomes a sodden, unwieldy hulk. Packs not lashed in may go riding off downwind to heaven knows where—or they may fill with water and sink. Some old-timers fasten packs in by unbuckling a shoulder strap, looping it over a thwart, and buckling it back to the pack. We use a section of nylon rope, criss-crossed over the packs and through the straps, culminating with a slip knot that can be tugged free if necessary. If a swamped canoe gets blown into a rocky, windswept shore, it may be necessary to get the packs out quick and lighten the hull before the waves mash it to pulp.

Lashing Packs In The Canoe

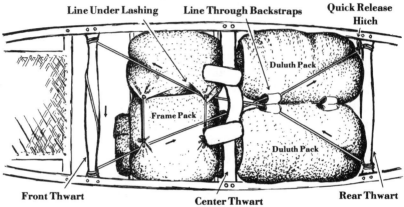

In some capsizing situations, especially with flat-bottom canoes, the craft does not go clear over but "kicks" sideways, dropping the paddlers into the water. If the passengers go out on the upwind side, the empty canoe may go sailing out of reach. In any capsize situation, it pays to grab the canoe when you go over and hang on. Some canoeists coil 15 feet of nylon line in the bow for an emergency "grab rope."

In the spring or fall, when the water temperature may be well below 50 degrees, swamping is not a very funny business. Survival time in the cold water may be anywhere from 5 to 10 minutes. At that time of the year it is prudent to travel within easy reach of the shore even though it may add a few miles. A spill in this situation means abandoning ship promptly, getting to the shore and out of the water. Since every canoeist should have dry matches in a pocket case, a fire can be started promptly and the paddler warmed up. If the air is fairly warm, the paddlers may get warmed up running down the shore chasing their overturned craft. But anyone thoroughly chilled and suffering uncontrollable shivering must be warmed quickly or hypothermia may send him into a stupor, convulsions, and death. A discussion of hypothermia will occur in a later chapter, but let it suffice for now to say that it is a very real cold-water threat.

Sometimes a person will run across a book that advises, "When waves get too big, a canoeist can simply lie down on the bottom and the natural buoyancy of the canoe will ride the waves out." Sure it will. Just how two paddlers with a canoe full of duffle are supposed to find a place to lie down is never explained, even if the idea would work. Furthermore, there is no reason to think a canoe would remain afloat just because some terrified paddler was stretched out in the bottom.

Frankly, we enjoy riding a good, howling wind, the canoe pitching and bucking with spray blowing off the tops of the whitecaps. But we know what we can handle and what we can't. When windbound, we brew up a pot of coffee, or maybe simply take a nap. Most of the time, winds will drop off before sunset; we get a good fix on direction and if need be, make up the distance in the stillness after dark.

Chapter 6

Fast Water

The old-timers have a saying: "Nobody ever drowned on a portage."It might also be added that few paddlers ever lost their canoe, tent, sleeping bags, cook kit, and food while taking a detour on foot around a set of rapids. But like the mountain climber who tackles the peak "because it's there," so the cruising canoeist sooner or later will point the nose of his craft into a stretch of white water. The choice is even easier for the canoeist. Rapids are all downhill.

While steelhead fishing in British Columbia with resident guide-angler-mountaineer Tim Timmins some years ago, we paused for a breather at the edge of a stream that elbowed, kicked, and bulled its way down to the Pacific in a spectacular stretch of thundering foam. "I wonder," I questioned aloud, "if a guy could run that in a canoe?"

"Yes, he could," said Tim thoughtfully. "Once."

And that is the literal truth about any set of rapids. They can be run—once. But there is no guaranteeing the condition of the canoe, outfit, or personnel at the exit. Shooting a stretch of current and froth can be an adrenaline-charged kick for an experienced paddler who knows his canoe and his own ability and can judge at a glance if there is a navigable route through. But the chances are he didn't learn his skills on a wilderness camping trip by risking a canoe-load of equipment. He learned in an empty canoe, with safety devices, and most probably with an experienced paddler.

It is not required that a cruising camper be a competition white-water expert. Few of us are. But he should have a working knowledge of how his craft reacts in a current, what paddle strokes are required to get through turbulent water, and an ability to "read" moving water, to accurately judge whether a given stretch can be safely run.

The ideal craft for white-water practice is smooth-bottomed, without a keel, ample of beam, high in buoyancy, and rockered fore and aft. Slick, tough fiberglass and plastic take the bangs well and slide over rocks easier than metal, which tends to grab and stick. Buoyancy is provided by length and width, flare, tumblehome, decking or partial decking, and good flotation. Rocker and a no-keel bottom allow the craft to be turned abruptly, even spun on its axis and slipped from side to side.

You say you don't own a white-water canoe? Well, we don't either. So we will get in the river with what we own because that is what we will be cruising in.

For protection we will all be wearing Personal Floatation Devices (PFDs). And if we can beg, borrow, or steal helmets, we will wear them because we don't want our skulls cracked under water. If it is the spring or fall, with cold water a certain prospect, we will get a couple of wet suits so we don't wind up hypothermia cases. And we will go with at least one more team of canoeists so we have somebody ashore or afloat for assistance if we really get into a bind.

O.K., all set? Let's push off, paddle to the middle of the stream, and head down-current. According to our map there is some kind of a drop ahead, but not a very steep one, so we are looking and listening for it. The first indication appears as a line across the water. As we look down the stream sides, we see trees, brush, and rocks coming down to the shore. But straight ahead, on that line across the water, we realize we are looking at the trees from a point on the trunk; the roots, brush, and shoreline rocks are below our vision. As we approach, we see a few flicks of foam or waves on the lip of the drop and we hear water gurgling. So we pick a nice flat place to land, pull over to the shore, and get out for a look.

What we have ahead is merely a riffle that drops down through some gravel deposits, just a nice current to ride down through. But wait a minute. What is that sound around the bend? We walk a little further and we see where the stream has now narrowed down and is pulsing through an array of boulders, a "rock garden" in river parlance. On the left side we note where the main force of the current is moving through a sufficiently deep, unobstructed channel; below that is a long stretch of quiet water.

Fine. Now we know we can float through that riffle, keep to the left, and pick up our route through the rock garden. We made a mental note that if we come through in low water, we would probably have to wade through there instead of riding.

Back in the canoe, we paddle to the main current, pick the "V" where the water enters the riffle, ride down to the left channel into the rock garden, and sail through—with just one loud thump as the hull connects with a submerged rock we didn't see from the shore. A fleeting glimpse shows some paint and aluminum on the rock, so ours isn't the first canoe that ever made contact there.

Ahead the river narrows and we see another line across the water, with quite a few little whiffs of spray bounding in the sunlight and a more insistent roar. And again we beach, get out, and take a look. Stretching nearly all the way across the stream is a level rock formation, a "ledge," which acts something like a dam. Water is shallow on top of the ledge. Where it drops in three feet below is a lot of turbulence, with the current washing back against the ledge. If we try to go over the ledge, we stand a good chance of getting stuck, broaching, and rolling over. If we clear the ledge, we wind up in that backwash below where we could get rolled around for some time. We don't buy that.

But on the near side of the ledge is a break in the rock, a "chute" where the main force of water is booming through. It is a straight, fast slick halfway down, but then in the middle there's a big boulder with the water piling up in front of it, bouncing over its top and churning away to the bottom in a series of foamy waves that merge with a row of "haystacks" or standing waves where the current ends its wild dash into quiet water.

O.K., we're on our way. We drop to our knees to lower our center of gravity, line up for the chute, and start down, having decided we will take the right side of the big rock. But wait a minute. As we start in, the current is moving us over in line with the rock. The bowman is paddling furiously to get right, and he does, but the current now has a good shot at the stern and the canoe is going down at an angle. The bow clears the rock, but the horrified stern man, flailing wildly, barely has time to yell, "Look out!" *Bam,* the craft hits, teeters momentarily, and then leans upstream, the river pours in over the upstream gunwale. In a flicker, canoe and paddlers are awash.

We have done our homework so we don't panic. We go out of the craft upstream so that the swamped hull with half a ton of water won't come crashing down to pin us against a rock below. And we have flipped over on our backs, heels downstream, so anything we hit will be cushioned by our feet and not our heads. A good thing, too, because we go clear under the foam momentarily, feel rocks ricocheting off our boots, before we bob up at the base of the haystacks. Our friends, who portaged around, are doubled up with mirth on the shore. But they eventually paddle out, retrieve our paddles, and help us tow our wallowing craft to the shore. If nothing else, we've learned a few things:

Grounded canoes do not usually "roll" over in a current. What happens is that the force of the current, passing under the hull, pulls the upstream gunwale down. That's the side that water pours into. We begin to understand why a keel canoe not only hangs rocks better but also gives the current more to work on when stuck. We've found out that we had better be lined up correctly as we move into the chute. If we're not, we can't correct our error by paddling faster across the current.

We also have found out that a life vest only provides buoyancy in "solid" water; in foam, a person will sink to the bottom, vest and all (which now explains why people who go over dams or ledges sometimes don't come up even though they were wearing PFDs). We wipe the water off our faces, dump out the canoe, carry it back up, and run the same stretch again.

This time, we line up a little better. But as we start moving toward the chute, we see that the current has a little side motion, drawing us to the left in line with that boulder again. So now we backpaddle, angling the stern slightly to the right so that the current pushes us to the right as we "ferry" sideways in the slick. Now that we have ferried right, we head 'er down, but doggone it, we got a little too far right and may pop the ledge. We've got to correct to the left—but not with forward strokes to "beat" the current. Oh, no. Instead, the bow paddler is prying or pushing the canoe left and the stern man is leaning out with a powerful draw to the left. The canoe skids sideways, still lined up with the current, zips past the rock, bounces over the haystacks, and slides into flat water. We did 'er.

So we rode down a little riffle, through a rock garden, and made a short drop through a chute. Big deal! Well, maybe not. But we had better be good at these before we get too adventurous. Often such innocuous little drops will tear a canoe apart.

Just a few miles from our cabin is a small piece of water called Splash Lake. At the outlet are the timbers remaining from an old log sluice, circa 1910 or so. A moderate flow of water goes 200 yards through riffles and rocks into Newfound Lake. Around this riffle is a well-used portage, which most people walk, but a few don't. Thirty feet below the sluice is a piece of underwater ledge. To avoid the ledge requires a sharp movement across the current. Some make it, some don't. Twice we have been there when luck went bad.

The first was a beautiful Old Town, less than two weeks old, according to the owner. Time was early May, high water, and pretty cold when I came upon the two young men loading their camping gear into the canoe at the foot of the sluice. Without trying to be too nosy, I suggested that maybe the portage was a little more secure. I was volubly assured that they knew exactly what they were doing, that they would "shoot across" the current to miss the ledge, and on and on. I sat down against a tree to observe.

With the bowman in place, the stern paddler pushed off with a mighty shove. But maybe not mighty enough. The canoe swept down, smacked the ledge sideways, filled, jammed between two rocks, and broke amidships. Other than some skinned knees and shins, the men were all right. I helped them retrieve their outfit. Since I had a motor, I hauled them and their outfit six miles to the public landing. They didn't talk much on the way in.

At exactly the same spot, about a year later, Lee Schumacher, our local druggist, and I were portaging through and saw two young men with a rental Grumman canoe from Bernie Carlson's Quetico-Superior Outfitters, preparing to make that same cross-current assault. Unable to dissuade them from their venture, I hurried to a point below and captured the event on my Nikon—the push-off, impact with the ledge, water pouring over the upstream gunwale, and baptism by immersion. Luckily, the water level was lower and the current slower. The canoe merely sustained a few dents. At the bottom, they dumped out the water, gathered their sodden belongings, loaded up, and paddled homeward. That isn't exactly the story they told Bernie when they got back, but that's how it happened.

The years we were in the outfitting business, Lil and I credited three canoes to that stretch, one a brand-new 15-foot Grumman that was totaled on its first trip. Anyone who didn't understand moving water would look at that stretch and swear it was a piece of cake. There is just that one little flaw in the ride, but it's an important flaw.

To most canoeists who have never been racked up in a chute, their imagination cannot grasp the terrific impact of a swamped canoe containing a half to three-quarters of a ton of water when it hits an underwater obstruction. A high-floating, dry canoe will usually bounce off a rock or log, but a swamped craft will break, tear, collapse, even wrap right around a rock like a strip of tinfoil. Hundreds of artifacts—bow sections, ribs and canvas, bits of fiberglass and aluminum, some only a year old—decorate North America's major canoe routes from Texas to the Arctic, attesting to the power of currents against swamped hulls.

But back to the river. When you cruise with camping gear aboard, the canoe will act somewhat more sluggish than when empty. For that reason, and because they don't want to risk their equipment, many canoeists portage the packs across and take the canoes through empty. We do this quite often in unfamiliar water, carrying the packs around the rapids while we scout them out, leaving the packs at the take out point below.

A few years back, Ontario guide-outfitter Bud Dickson and I were on the Turtle River south of Bending Lake, a stream with some pretty fair drops, perhaps two-thirds of them runable. One of these sticks out in my mind, not because it was particularly difficult, but because of the variety of water.

From the top it eased off gradually, glassy and smooth, tilted into a rock garden that curved to the right, then poured into a small pool, with a fast, narrow chute going out 90 degrees left in a boil of foam and waves. We figured we would ship water in the rock garden and would need to make the eddy on the right, empty out, then cross over and pop the left edge of the chute to miss the worst of the turbulence. And that's how we played it. We glanced off a few donnickers coming down the rock garden, shipped two inches of slop, hit the current at the bottom with me leaning hard on a downstream brace, Bud digging for the bank, made an eddy turn, beached, and emptied out the liquid ballast. Going back into the current, we leaned downstream (remember, that current going under the hull pulls the upstream gunwale down) until we lined up with the chute, went off the lip of the drop, and shot through the left edge of the turbulence, the standing waves towering higher than our heads on the starboard gunwale. In the calm below, we moved in and picked up the packsacks.

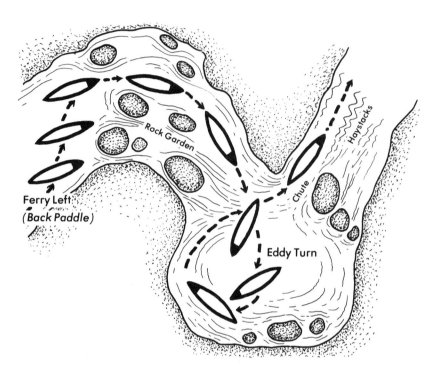

Before we rode that piece, we had looked it over together and were in complete agreement on what we would do. Had there been a disagreement, we would have carried around. There is no time to debate in the middle of a chute.

"Fine," says the guy from Iowa or Indiana or Illinois. "Now we have read about negotiating rapids, but down in this flat corn and soybean country, where do we find that kind of water to practice in?" Ah, but there are some rapids—and some beauts. In March and April, when spring rains fill the ditches and come boiling out of the drain tiles, those little meandering cow-pasture creeks turn into raging torrents with plenty of Class II and III rapids. I grew up on those Illinois farm flats southwest of Chicago, and we spent each spring riding down the Fox, DuPage, Kankakee, Ausable, DesPlaines, Hickory, and a few other streams, dodging iron fence posts, ferrying to miss bridge abutments, making eddy turns behind corn cribs, drawing and prying past hog feeders, egg crates, hay balers, dead livestock, and—as they say at the farm auctions—"other items too numerous to mention."

The Ausable, a summertime Dr. Jekyll, was a frothy Mr. Hyde in March. Doug Brown, from Minooka, and I lost a 17-foot Dow magnesium canoe there in 1950 when a sharp sliver of concrete from an old roadbed reached up and opened the bottom of our boat like a sardine can. That was almost 30 years ago, and I can still feel that icy water hitting my belly button. Anyway, the canoeist who really wants to learn about currents and chutes can find something almost anywhere in North America unless he lives in the middle of the Mojave.

The American Canoe Association Book Service lists some excellent white-water books for the cruiser as well as the serious downriver racer. One river book we have found informative is Peter Dwight Whitney's *Whitewater Sport,* published by Ronald Press.

Nearly all of the canoe manufacturers make keelless "white-water" models, some of which are true river boats and some just called river boats. Some companies specialize in white-water equipment—PFDs, helmets, waterproof equipment bags, paddles, wet suits, knee pads—and these include: Sea Suits, P.O. Box 245, Costa Mesa, Calif. 92627; Seda Products, P.O. Box 41B, San Ysidro, Calif. 92073; Extra Sport, P.O. Box 22, Halesite, N.Y. 11743; Phoenix Products, Inc., U.S. Route 421, Tyner, Kentucky 40486; Rocky Mountain Kayak Supply, P.O. Box 8150, Aspen, Colo. 81611, and Wayfarer Recreational Products, 1208 E. Elm Street, Springfield, Mo. 65802.

It should not be necessary to point out that anytime the loaded canoe is in a current, the gear should be lashed securely to the thwarts. But we have seen odds and ends of packs, bags, boots, and even loose life vests bounding downstream when someone spilled above. We use the same criss-cross lashing described for rough water in Chapter 5, with a quick-release knot at the stern thwart.

In a spill, with the gear lashed in, the whole package will hang together until it can be beached. In the event the canoe is jammed in the current, the slip knot can be yanked and the packs removed one at a time to help lighten the swamped craft.

There are other means of negotiating currents, of course, including lining and poling. The people we know line upstream, not down. This method of avoiding a portage is accomplished by lashing a single quarter-inch nylon rope to two points on the canoe, preferably one end to a bow ring and the other end to the stern thwart. In moderate current and along not too rugged a shore, one man can handle the single line. Otherwise, two ropes are used with two men working the canoe forward in steps. The trick is to let the bow swing into the current, then curb it so the bowline has a trifle more length than the stern line, keeping the canoe angled slightly into the current with both lines taut as the canoe is moved forward. Pressure on your arms will determine if the current is too swift. If so, slack off the stern line slightly. Then swing the bow into shore and carry the canoe over.

One Man Lining Upstream

Lining downstream is extremely precarious, since you have no real way to gauge the power of the current until the canoe is out there. If the pull is too strong to handle, one of two things happens, both of them bad: the canoeists let go of the ropes and the canoe goes wildcatting down the chute, end for end; or, either or both canoeists try to hang onto the rope and get yanked off the shore to go wildcatting down the chute along with the canoe—but not in it. Where they wind up and in what condition is anybody's guess. We always figure that if we can't ride the canoe down a rapids, we don't try to sneak it through on a rope. We carry around.

Poling, rivermen tell me, is more ancient than paddling, since primitive man probably pushed his log rafts around with sticks long before he figured out how to carve a paddle. In any event, this prehistoric method is now a highly developed art that is experiencing a considerable comeback in those areas where shallow streams abound. In the 1930s, I lived my summers on

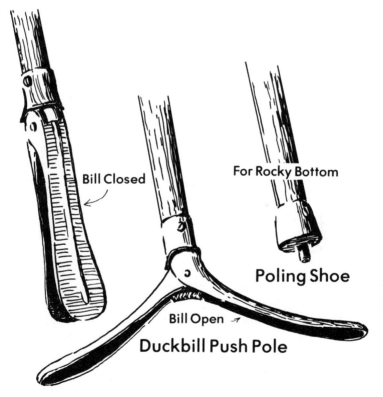

Bill Closed

For Rocky Bottom

Poling Shoe

Bill Open

Duckbill Push Pole

Illinois' Fox River, fetching and carrying for a maiden aunt schoolteacher who had a cottage two miles downriver from the village of Yorkville. My mode of transportation was an 18-foot

Old Town Guide Model, which I poled up to Yorkville and downstream to Sheridan and back. By trial and error, sheer luck, and some wet clothes, I learned how to stand back of the center thwart, one leg braced against the stern thwart, the other forward, the iron-shod point of the pole trailing for a series of quick jabs or a long push where I planted the pole and then "climbed" it, hand over hand. Coming downstream, I learned to balance, using the pole for direction, or in a fast section, to use it as a brake against the bottom, "snubbing" and letting the canoe down the current a little at a time.

In some areas of North America, particularly the Northeast, poling is still the accepted way of moving freight or a camping outfit on a stream. Recreational poling, on the other hand, has jumped in popularity with competition races even being held in some areas. For a comprehensive account, get the book *Canoe Poling* by Al, Syl and Frank Beletz, put out by the A. C. Mackenzie Press, Box 9301, Richmond Heights Station, St. Louis, Mo. 63117. Drop them a postcard for current price.

There is another type of poling popular in the North, and that is with a duckbilled pole used for harvesting rice. We acquire the aluminum "duckbills" from Herters at Waseca, Minnesota, and fix them to the end of a 12-foot sapling. When the pole is pulled ahead, the hinged bill collapses. When the bill is pushed into the mud bottom, it spreads out, offering a base to push against. We harvest rice in September using a cleanly scrubbed 17-foot Grumman with the middle thwart removed to make a more convenient opening for the rice to land in. We work together, Lil kneeling just ahead of the thwart, "pounding" the rice with the two light 30-inch wooden flails, me standing behind, steadily forcing the bow through the greenish brown stalks. As the canoe moves ahead with the bow raised slightly, Lil reaches forward with the right flail and draws a bunch of stalks over the right gunwale, then taps the heads with a scissoring motion of the left flail, knocking the ripe rice into the canoe. Leaning to the left, she pulls stalks over the left gunwale with the left flail and taps the grain off with the right flail. And so on, back and forth, in rapid rhythm.

Our Ojibwa neighbors from Nett Lake and Lake Vermillion **can pound out 90 to 200 pounds of rice per canoe per day. Lil** and I average about 50, but we only harvest enough to carry us through the winter—a little vegetable matter to bolster our roast mallards or venison tenderloin and to provide a cushion for the orange-juice gravy.

Chapter 7

The Motor Canoe

Way back in 1909, a Milwaukee engineer by the name of Ole Evinrude assembled the first practical outboard motor, a device hailed as a boon to the rowboat fisherman. It was only a matter of months before a diehard canoeist sawed two feet of canvas and planking off the stern of his paddle craft, added a transom, and started a new phase of canoeing. The motor canoe, square-back or side-bracket, is the aquatic pickup truck of the fisherman, hunter, trapper, freighter.

There are, of course, drawbacks to motorized canoe use, one of which is added weight. Square-backs weigh from one-fourth to one-half more than paddle craft. Motors run from 24 pounds for a two-horse up to 50 or more for a bigger power plant; and five gallons of gas will weigh 40 pounds. However much gas it takes to get someplace, it takes the same amount to get back. Even with a side-bracket on a paddle canoe, the weight difference of motor and gas is considerable. But a lot of people use 'em. At least 25 canoe makers in North America currently turn out some 38 models of square sterns and "T" backs, and there's no count on the number of paddle canoes that are sometimes fitted with brackets.

Matching the motor to the canoe is as important as matching the canoe to the job. In Canada's far north, Cree trappers and freighters have long used big Peterboro square-backs with 10-horsepower plants, and they portage these outfits all over. But then, we have seen these same individuals pack over 400 pounds up a Hudson Bay Company loading dock. In a few emergencies, we have used a 10-horse on a 17-foot square-back, but on a regular canoe this motor is unstable.

Orville "Porky" Meyers of Lansing, Iowa, and Harry "Ponce" DeLeon of Moline, Illinois, a pair of motor-canoe specialists who have fished and hunted every nook and cranny of the Mississippi River from Muscatine to Dubuque, used a modified 17-foot Grumman with a 10-horse Johnson outboard. They built a V-shaped aluminum plate that was riveted to the keel, under the stern. The wings of the "V" extended beyond the motor shaft. This rig raised the stern, under power, in such a way that the canoe barely skimmed the surface. Not only did this combination fly at a teeth-chattering 30 mph, but when Orville and Harry wished to cross a Mississippi sandbar to another channel, they simply hit wide open and "jumped" across. The one ride I had with these daredevils was sufficient, and I do not advocate big motors on small canoes. However, these two knew exactly what they were doing. As far as I know, they are still doing it.

A big motor, besides making a canoe stern-heavy and difficult to maneuver, tends to drag the canoe down if it swamps. I have never seen flotation comparisons on motor-canoe sizes, but manufacturers would be providing a service if they listed motor weights that will float with their craft. Most guides and outfitters prefer something in the 4-hp. or under category. For light, fast travel, Lil and I like the 2-horse with an integral tank, handier on portages than the remote tank with a hose. With careful use, we get over 20 miles per gallon on the 2-horse.

The old-style square-stern is squat in the back and has considerable drag. It's a bummer to paddle. The new "T" sterns with their sharp taper are easier to paddle, but they're not as easy to maneuver under power. Style here is a matter of personal preference. On trips where we will be doing considerable paddling along with motor use, we prefer a side-bracket-mounted motor on a regular double-end canoe.

In heavy winds, power canoes allow the pilot to concentrate on his seamanship without the fatigue of swinging a paddle. This is an important point with the solo traveler who can cover water he could never navigate by arm power. But I do *not* mean that motor canoes are foolproof in rough water. You need as much skill to handle a power canoe in heavy waves as you do a paddle craft. And if the motor quits, it's prayer time. Side-bracket motors tend to throw water into the stern in a heavy sea. Also they steer somewhat differently, since the motor is alongside the stern seat, has a pivoting effect at that point, and doesn't respond as quickly when you want to make a sharp turn.

In river currents, outboards sometimes do strange things on square-backs as well as side mounts. When you're heading upstream, turbulence tends to yank the motor from side to side. It pays to have an alert bowman with a paddle when you're climbing around obstacles. You must carefully pick the deepest slot in a chute to avoid prop contact with a rock. A sheared pin and immediate loss of power can cause a sideways skid and a spill. Similarly, smacking an underwater obstacle under full power can flip the canoe.

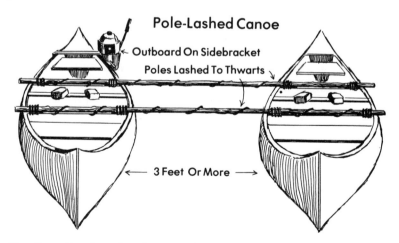

Pole-Lashed Canoe

← Outboard On Sidebracket

Poles Lashed To Thwarts

← 3 Feet Or More →

On the other hand, when you're fishing or cruising slowly, the shaft hanging down creates an initial stability somewhat like a continual paddle brace.

One motor is often used to move two or more canoes. Even a small "eggbeater" can hustle along a side-lashed pair or three in tandem like a string of frankfurters. When you're towing tandem, you should tie only the stern rope firmly. Each trailing canoe has its bowline lashed to the spare paddle, wedged under the deck brace. In the event of an emergency, you flip the paddle overboard, freeing the towed canoe. Also, when several canoes are pulled in tandem, the stern man in the last canoe must usually "rudder" to keep the line straight.

Side-by-side towing involves lashing poles across the thwarts to hold the craft three feet or more apart. We use dry, dead fir or spruce. If one canoe is a square-back without a stern thwart, the rear pole will be lashed to angle from the center of the square-back to the stern thwart of the paddle canoe. The three-foot-plus interval between the canoes is necessary to allow waves to pass between without either craft shipping water. A slight toe-in of the two bows will also help eliminate slop.

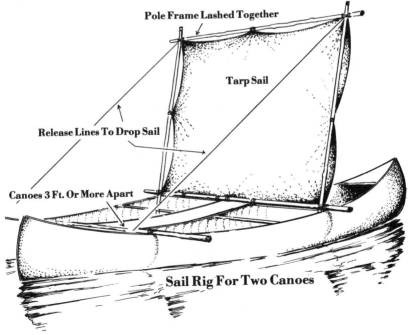

Pole Frame Lashed Together

Tarp Sail

Release Lines To Drop Sail

Canoes 3 Ft. Or More Apart

Sail Rig For Two Canoes

This same side-by-side rig is used for sailing with the wind. A frame of four poles is lashed to form a mast frame, the bottom "boom" resting across the gunwales, the top roped upright. A tarp is tied to form a square sail and the crew sacks out while one man rudders.

A word of caution about side-lashed canoes. They are initially quite stable, like a pontoon boat. But in rough water they are not as seaworthy together as alone and can give a false sense of security. They are not much good at all in white water. As a casting platform in still water they are excellent, and stand-up fishermen can ply their skill with ease. When four people fish from this setup, however, care must be taken not to perforate somebody's ear on a backcast. In traveling any distance with side-by-side craft, we lash each pole with a single line, half-hitched to pole and thwart from gunwale to gunwale across the bows, gunwale to gunwale across both sterns. Tied off with slip knots, each section can be broken down and reassembled in moments at a portage.

Lashing Two Canoes Together

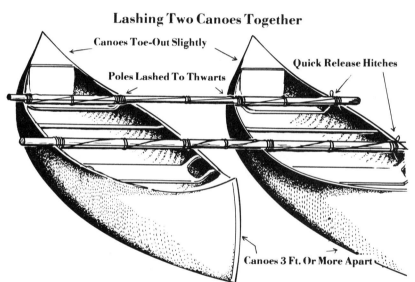

Canoes Toe-Out Slightly

Quick Release Hitches

Poles Lashed To Thwarts

Canoes 3 Ft. Or More Apart

When making the ties, we have found it expedient to lash the left-hand canoe with the pole to the bow thwart, push it offshore, shove the right-hand canoe under the pole, lash it, and then tie in the rear pole, starting on the left and moving right.

Guides say that any motor is only as good as the tool kit. Trouble must be anticipated and maintenance procedure understood. Any canoeist who motors into the bush without at least a nodding acquaintance with his power plant is apt to return by paddle through a fog of profanity.

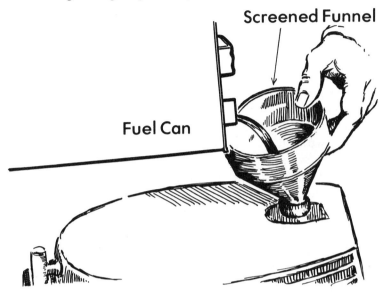

Two trouble spots are the motor itself and the fuel, with about a 50-50 chance that either or both may create problems. Fuel should be mixed fresh in clean, tightly capped containers. A fine-mesh funnel is indispensable to keep dirt, bits of metal, and water out of the motor tank. Metal funnels do not float, so a piece of nylon line tied through a hole punched in the rim of the funnel and then fastened to a gas-can handle is a good precaution.

Water in a gas can may not be apparent immediately, since the water will sink to the bottom of the can and usually doesn't start pouring out until the can is two-thirds empty. A few drops of water may go right through a hot motor with an asthmatic cough or two, but any more than a couple of drops will foul the plugs and stop the motor cold. Water in a can may be spotted with a flashlight. It looks like a flat bubble rolling around the bottom. In a gas-ration situation, the "good" gas can be slowly poured off the top of the contaminated can, through a funnel into a clean container, and the last watery residue dumped on the rocks well back from shore where it will evaporate and vanish.

There are occasions when a motor canoe may swamp. Unloading a light canoe with a side mount may result in an imbalance so the craft rolls over near shore. One way to beat this hazard is to remove the motor first, before the packs are taken out. Another is to beach broadside with the motor inshore, the prop resting on solid ground. If a canoe rolls over in the water with a nonoperating motor, it can usually be righted and the motor started up. If the motor is running, however, water may be sucked into the inside, which means that the carburetor, fuel line, and tank must be cleaned and dried out. A hot motor hitting cold water may also crack the head or blow the head gasket. It doesn't pay to roll over, especially with the power on.

To clean a waterlogged motor, start by dumping out anything in the gas tank (not in the water, please). Unscrew the drain plug on the carburetor, and pour some fresh gas into the tank. It will run through the fuel line and out the drain hole, cleaning out any water. Unscrew the spark plugs, slosh some fresh gas into the cylinders, and turn the motor upside down and drain it out. With new spark plugs installed, fresh gas in the tank, and the carburetor plug in tight, the motor should kick off.

A tool kit for the motor will include adjustable pliers, screwdriver, extra spark plugs, extra shear pins, an extra cotter pin, coil of wire, piece of emery cloth for cleaning plugs, and a roll of tape. Some guides tape a couple of spare shear pins to the steering handle of the outboard.

Prior to the trip, the motor should be tuned. Every north-country outfitter has seen canoeists load up at the dock, gas their outboard, set the spark, pull out the choke and then pull the starter cord—and pull, and pull, and pull. And a whole lot of pulls. This is usually accompanied by the comment, "Well, it was running good when I put it away last fall." Uh-huh. Or, "My cousin said it was running good when he loaned it to me."

In a twin-cylinder motor, you'll notice a distinct drop in power and a change in the sound if one cylinder cuts out. In a single-cylinder motor the difference is even more distinct: silence. It takes only a moment to pull the wires, remove the plugs with the adjustable pliers, and put in new ones. The old plugs can be cleaned up at camp and put in the tool kit.

Sometimes the recoil spring on the starter will snap. In this case, unscrew the cowl, remove the rewind and stuff it into a pack, and start the motor manually with a rope. If a motor "freezes up," it is usually because somebody didn't mix oil in the gas. Stuck pistons, after they cool, can be loosened by removing the spark plugs, pouring a little raw gas into each cylinder, and tapping the top of each piston with a hardwood stick through the spark-plug hole, alternately pulling on the starter cord. Regassed with the proper mixture, the motor should run O.K.

Another trouble sign is a grinding sound with a jerking on the shaft, an indication that the lower gearbox may have no grease. It is essential when starting a trip to check the lower unit, grease it, and make sure the grease plugs are in tight. One very common method of accidentally degreasing the lower unit is by getting monofilament line wrapped in the propeller. This generally occurs when you're trolling forward and the canoe runs over the line. The nylon coil bunches between the prop and the soft-brass grease seal, chews through the grease seal, and allows the grease to escape. When the grease goes from the lower unit, the gears destruct and the trip becomes a paddle-only enterprise.

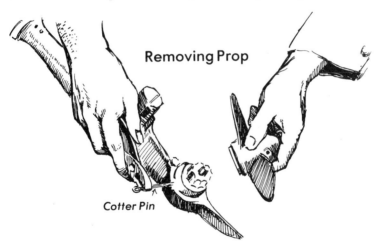

Removing Prop

Cotter Pin

A broken shear pin is indicated when the motor begins to race and forward progress stops. Most small motors are equipped with a clutch arrangement so that when an underwater obstacle hits the prop, the prop disengages rather than tearing off a blade. As a further safeguard, most motors are equipped with a soft-brass shear pin, which passes through a slot in the prop shaft that corresponds with a slot in the prop housing. A hard impact will snap the pin, freeing the prop before the blades or the motor shaft get damaged. Replacing a shear pin requires removal of the prop cap, cotter pin, prop nut, and prop. The broken pin will be partly inside the prop housing and partly in the shaft. The piece in the shaft can be tapped out with the new pin as it is set in place, and the prop remounted.

During any repair procedure, the canoe should be beached. Motor surgery should be handled on dry land, preferably over a tarp so that loose parts won't get into the sand. Attempting to repair a motor out in the water may result in some essential part accidentally getting the deep six.

If somebody forgets the extra shear pins or the supply runs out, a substitute is required. In a pinch we have used a piece of wire or the shank from a large fishhook. I have heard of motors being run at low speed with a matchstick for a shear pin, but we have never tried it.

The last major problem with an outboard, and one that may sound ridiculous, is loss of the motor altogether. This might seem impossible, but it happens often. These losses occur when the motor, not screwed tight to the transom or side mount, jumps off and disappears. Anyone with a lick of sense uses a chain, cable, or rope safety line to secure the motor to the canoe. This precaution will keep the outboard from vanishing entirely, but it won't keep it from coming off the mount if the screws are loose.

Twice in 40 years I have had motors come off canoe mounts. One was a little 1½-horse that went off a square stern on a sharp turn. I managed to retain hold of the steering handle while I cut the spark with my other hand. The second was a two-cylinder 4-horse that came off a side mount like a howling banshee and wound up in my lap, the whirling prop hanging over the left gunwale. It took only a frantic moment to shut this off, too. Lil noted that this was a novel way to liven up an otherwise dull day, but I don't look forward to any more such episodes.

Chapter 8

Home on the Shoreline

A rolling line of greenish black clouds wiped out the sun and blackened the surface of Manitoba's Nelson River as a tree-bending gale howled through the spruce forest. A dozen Cree women and kids, scattering to the shelter of their cabins on the far shore, were suddenly blotted from view by the driving rain.

There was a momentary gasp, as though the whole outdoors had sucked in its breath. Then the full fury of the storm smacked our tent, yanking frantically on the guy ropes and probing to find a line, flap, or peg that could be pulled loose or pried up. Luckily, the advance buildup of towering thunderheads and the shattering crack of lightning bolts playing off the granite shield had given ample warning that a real belly buster was bearing down. Pegs secure, guy lines tight, our fabric shelter swayed with the bending spruce but weathered the battering blasts.

Inside, Lil had a candle lit, a flickering yellow symbol of cheer that buoyed our spirits like a thumb to the nose against the fury outside. Our daughter Barb rearranged the sacked sleeping bags in a triangle of seats, broke open the food pack, and passed around a snack of sausage, cheese, and Rye Krisp. We rode out the storm, secure behind those few yards of nylon that separated us from all the power nature could unleash.

There was a time when a furious thunderstorm was no cause for mirth on the canoe trails. Big, square-wall tents could be uprooted from their moorings or simply blown flat. Extreme care had to be exercised not to touch the inside of the "waterproof" canvas lest the air seal be broken and rain pour through. In a driving wind, rain often poured through anyway. If it didn't come through the top, it would run down the sides and come racing across the floor. Troops of mosquitos sought out gaps between the front flaps or between the side walls and the ground cloth, infiltrating to add another dimension of discomfort.

But with today's tightly woven synthetic material, zippered insect-proof doorway, waterproof floor and rain fly, there is no valid reason for any camper to experience much discomfort from either weather or bugs. The revolution in tent materials has been matched with some sound research on what makes a tent a tent, with the result that designers have gone back to the steep-roofed "A" style and "pyramid" shape that served nomads and expeditions from the time of Alexander the Great to the Civil War. The so-called wall tent, strictly an American rag-barn construction, along with its various mutations such as the "Baker," was about as lightweight and handy as hauling a tar-paper shack on a canoe trip. Thank goodness they are gone.

A good synthetic-fiber four-man canoe tent today weighs under ten pounds, complete with poles and pegs. It is self-supporting, well ventilated, and bug-proof. It rolls up about the size of a big loaf of bread. Furthermore, it is easier to erect, requires much less maintenance, and has a longer life expectancy than any canvas tent that ever existed. That is, a *good* synthetic-fiber tent. Beware of *bad* synthetic-fiber tents that are not much more than sunshades. No canoe camper should wind up with a bum shelter unless he gets suckered in on some cut-rate gimmick. The boom in camping has also created a boom in hustlers peddling schlock outdoor gear, so let's take a look at what constitutes a good tent.

Most experienced canoeists prefer a two-piece shelter: an inner tent of lightweight "breathable" material covered by a separate, tough, waterproof rain fly. The reason for the separate fly is that any material that is made waterproof outside is usually waterproof inside. Moisture can't get out. Every person sleeping in a tent overnight exudes about one pint of water through breathing and perspiration. There is no way to shut this water off; it is simply oozing out of us all the time. If this moisture cannot get out of the tent, it will condense on the interior fabric and drip down, in effect causing "rain" inside the tent. Sleeping bags, clothing, cameras, packs, and toilet articles all get damp and soggy. Most tents, even the cheesy ones, have some sort of ventilation, front and back, so they can be left open in good weather. But during a driving rain, when the flaps are tied shut, a good tent's porous fabric, plus ventilators in protected areas such as the peak ends, will remove interior wetness while the waterproof fly is keeping the rain off outside.

A waterproof floor that extends up the sides from 8 to 12 inches will keep groundwater from entering. Sewn-in mosquito-proof doors bar insects. Suspension systems of jointed metal or fiberglass keep the tent and fly erect while an integrated peg and guy-rope system anchor it securely. And the whole outfit can be assembled or taken down in minutes.

One of the earliest A-shaped canoe tents made of nylon was designed by our neighbor, Sandy Bridges, resident director of the Boy Scout base just up the shore. Bridges, a veteran guide, trapper, and canoeman, tested just about every tent design in North America before he developed his own prototype now widely used by the Boy Scout organization under the label "Adventure I" or "Nylon Voyageur." It is a modified A design, 7½ x 8½ feet with 66 inches of height and with a urethane-coated floor lapped 18 inches up the sides. Walls and top are nylon taffeta, and the fly is urethane-coated rip-stop. Suspension is by outside 3-joint aluminum poles front and back. This tent holds up to four persons, weighs about 8½ pounds, and is moderately priced.

A very popular canoe tent put out by the Eureka Tent Co., Inc., 625 Conklin Rd., Binghamton, N.Y. 13902, is called the Timberline. This 8-pound, 14-ounce, four-man shelter measures 7'2" × 8'9", has a 58-inch peak and costs about the same as the Adventure I. Eureka also makes a superlite (6-pound, 15-ounce) two-man tent with floor dimensions of 5'3" × 7'2" and a 42-inch peak that is more modestly priced. For cold weather, we use an 8' × 8' Alpine Designs, Boulder, Colo., centerpole model with two doors, tunnel, and cook hole. I do not know what these excellent tents sell for now, but they aren't cheap.

North Face, 1234 Fifth St., Berkeley, Calif. 94710, manufactures a top grade, two-man A-frame called the Sierra with a floor area measuring 7'9" × 4'8" and a 48-inch peak. It is fairly expensive.

Some other fine tents, designed for backpacking but adaptable to canoeing are made by the Paul Petzoldt Co., Box 78, Lander, Wyo. 82520. Paul, of National Outdoor Leadership School fame, is no longer connected with the company, but his designs are still there. Holubar, Box 7, Boulder, Colo. 80302, has a 4-man, 8' × 8' centerpole expedition model weighing 12 pounds. Gerry, at 5450 North Valley Highway, Denver, Colo. 80216, offers a family of A-frames aimed at tough weather conditions. Anyone handy with a sewing machine can acquire a fine tent in kit form from Frostline, Dept. C, 452 Burbank, Broomfield, Colo. 80020, priced between the Adventure I and the Sierra.

Owning a good tent is only part of the package. Putting it up correctly is the other part. Most tent sites on North American canoe routes are used over and over by successive campers because they are the best sites available—sometimes the only ones. Many of these sites were in use before the arrival of Europeans, by generations of Iroquois, Algonquin, Abanaki, Cree, Chippewayan, and their kinfolk. Most of these are essentially warm-weather sites, on exposed points and islands where a breeze will keep insects away. Protected, interior winter camping areas are harder to find. They have grown over with brush to a great extent and their use is discouraged by forestry personnel who must consider the fire potential. Since most of the canoe cruising is in warm weather, let's check out what constitutes a good summer site.

We look for a smooth, flat area, free of protruding rocks or roots, on a raised or sloping situation where rainwater won't collect, shadowed by a few low pines, spruce, fir, or by birch or other hardwoods. Those scenic, needle-carpeted sites beneath towering pines may look and smell good, but those big trees often act like lightning rods in a thunderstorm. It is safer to sleep under a 23,000-volt powerline than under those needled attractors. We have seen the results of lightning strikes on camps, not only on the

tree and ground beneath but on people tenting there. The lucky
ones came off stunned, perhaps slightly scorched. On the other
hand, we know of a half-dozen over the last decade who were
transferred from various campsites in canvas sacks. Sometimes
those needled lightning rods show the scars of past strikes: vertical
slices in the bark, limbs blown off the top. In the granite-shield
country of the north, you don't have to be under the tree to get
jarred, only nearby. The juice travels a long way underground.

Most campsites slope a little, and we usually aim the tent with
the front downhill. That's because we usually sleep with our feet
toward the door. It's a good idea to sleep with your feet level with
or slightly lower than your head. If your head is lower than your
feet, you're likely to wake up with a headache or nausea—if you
get to sleep at all.

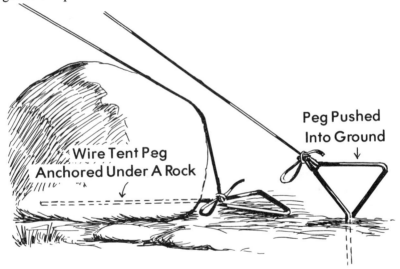

Hardly anyone cuts his own tent stakes anymore since this is a
no-no in parks and designated wilderness areas. Among the best
lightweight metal pegs we have used are those made of stiff wire
with a triangular-shaped end loop. They are 9 inches long, can be
pushed into mineral soil straight down or angled (if there is ledge
below), or they can be hooked to a tent loop and anchored with a
big rock. Where bedrock is on the surface, a section of a blow-
down "rolled in" parallel to the side of the tent will make a good
anchor for tent-fly guy lines.

It is always a fair assumption that it may storm, even if the evening is clear and the stars glitter calmly overhead. While daylight remains, the shelter should be guyed out to accommodate an unexpected gale. Wind can do funny things. Once, a thousand campsites ago in the era of canvas tents, Lil and I were pitching our pearl-gray Bemis when a sudden squall struck. This shelter had an inner aluminum-pole frame that allowed it to be erected as a unit. When the first gust hit, neither of us had a good grip on a guy rope. With a whoosh, our fabric home went airborne like a big box kite and probably would have set a new soaring record if a gnarled jackpine hadn't reached out and arrested its flight. I climbed the tree and managed to tug down the tent while Lil and our two kids howled with laughter.

Another wind hazard is a weak, rotten tree hovering over the campsite, the classic "widow maker." A glance around any campsite with even an unpracticed eye will reveal a leaning tree caught temporarily in the upper story of a neighbor, or one with leaves or needles gone, waiting for the right gust to send it crashing earthward like a king-sized deadfall. Nobody has to camp under one of these hazards. If it cannot be pulled down or shaken down, avoid the site.

Jointed tent poles come with plastic or rubber stoppers for the bottom section, which helps keep them from sinking into sand or mud. These stoppers also keep sand and mud from working up inside the pole like a plug. In soft situations, or where the stopper has been lost, a bit of old bark or log heeled into the turf will keep the pole from sinking.

Fires should be built nowhere but on dirt, sand, or rock. Every book, pamphlet, or folder on the subject tells the fire builder the same thing. Yet forest fires are still ignited every year by campers who locate their hearth on loose forest floor duff, or start a fire against a dry stump that sucks up flames like a chimney, or under overhanging conifers that go off like Roman candles. The cook site must be where the fire cannot burn down, around, or up—or be blown into trouble. In wet situations, a lightweight, urethane-coated kitchen fly is a welcome addition. You can cook and eat under the fly if you keep the fire small, or if you use a lightweight stove. In prolonged wet-wood situations or in areas where firewood is scarce, a compact stove may be the best choice.

Most kitchen flies are made with corner grommets so they can be slung with ropes like a pitched roof. Another method is to have a grommet sunk in the center of the tarp (with some additional reinforcing tapes to the corners) so that the fly can be hung by a center rope tossed over an overhanging limb and then guyed out.

Once the tent is up and secured, the next concern is sanitation. Of course, if the paddlers have been pushing hard for a number of hours, this concern may have a higher priority. We usually scout the area, determine where any previous campers built their biffy, cover any remains, and build our own. We seek a spot where a smooth dead-wood pole can be lashed between two trees for a seat, a second pole higher up on the opposite side of the trunks for a backrest, and a situation where a section of the forest floor can be carefully lifted out, set aside, and later replaced when we leave. Loose dirt is set in a neat pile to be sprinkled on each "job" to anchor the paper. Some top-notch campers take the paper back to the fire and burn it. When leaving the campsite, the poles are taken down, the sod restored, and all signs of use obliterated. Human waste in a shallow situation is soon reduced by insects and bacteria and absorbed by surrounding vegetation.

With the tent, fireplace, and biffy secure, the next concern is a good supply of water and fuel. Over most of the north, a continual source of drinking water is passing under the canoe all day, but it is good to check in advance with U.S. or Canadian government authorities. Water purification tablets are handy but not necessarily 100 percent foolproof. For instance, they will not counteract pulp-plant acid. By boiling water for ten minutes you will kill a lot of impurities, but maybe not chemical problems. Health authorities have one sure test for drinking water: If you don't know for sure, don't drink it. Knowledge *before* the trip is essential.

Also, even in remote areas where water is relatively pure, there can be problems along the shoreline in hot weather. On still days, shoreline water is often crawling with an assortment of tiny beasties, some of which may raise havoc in an intestinal tract. We paddle out from shore and get our water, and use purification tablets when we have the slightest doubt.

Firewood is seldom a problem in remote areas, except possibly the Arctic. Where there is frequent use, campsites may be picked clean. Rather than disfigure the site by tearing or chopping lower dead limbs off live trees, experienced campers will paddle up the shore and gather enough cooking-size wood for their stay. Even in wet weather, relatively dry wood is available from standing dead saplings in the thick, sheltered part of the forest. Much has been made about what kinds of wood make the best blaze, but it is of little value to know that hickory makes a nice hot fire when scrub spruce is the only wood available. We use whatever is around, hardwoods or conifers, in small amounts for cooking. The old-time campfire, the roaring inferno that required a long-handled frying pan to cook fish and was also used to drive away evil spirits, is fast fading into oblivion. Failure to keep fires small can lead to the outlawing of all wood fires, which has occurred in some areas. In those places, all cooking must be done on portable stoves.

All of the foregoing—rainproof, bug-proof tent; water; cooking fire—lead to bedtime, which finally centers on sleeping gear. No other element of camping equipment has advanced faster than designs of durable, warm, light, compact and reasonably priced sleeping systems that now cover a thermal spectrum from temperate to Arctic.

The bedding breakthrough began in the 1930s with the advent of low-priced kapok bags, crude by today's standards, but an improvement over a roll of blankets held together by safety pins and less expensive than a sleeping bag of wool batting. There were some very expensive goose-down bags on the market at that time, but the average camper never saw one, much less slept in one.

During World War II, thousands of U.S. servicemen, many of them also outdoorsmen, were exposed to various GI sleeping robes, among them lightweight duck-down and feather sacks that were fairly comfortable even though the feathers that "leaked" during the night had to be plucked from the underwear in the morning.

In the 1950s and 60s the race between down and synthetic fiber was being run in earnest with a multi-million-dollar camping market at stake. Nobody won the race, but the competition spawned the most comfortable assortment of sleeping gear available to humans since Adam sought shelter under a leaf.

Currently, there is controversy between advocates of top-grade down and the users of the leading synthetics—Celanese Polar-Guard,® Dupont Fiberfil® II and Hollofil® II, and 3M Thinsulate,® although the latter is primarily used for clothing. There is certainly no agreement among the 30-odd outfitters who operate around the Superior–Quetico area where I live, except that a quality synthetic bag is usually lower-priced than one of quality down. Currently, Lil and I own both goose down and synthetic bags, using the down in cold/dry situations, synthetics in warm/wet.

Goose down offers the most insulation for the weight and is most compressible for packsack storage. It is also expensive and is susceptible to moisture. A wet down bag is like a sack of soggy oatmeal, and it's the dickens to dry out. In winter search-and-rescue work, we have seen frozen feet, the result of down bags getting soaked up by melting snow or condensation. Veteran campers who prefer down bags say, "Don't get your bag wet, dummy." Good advice, no matter what material you use.

Synthetic-fiber bags, even when wet, retain much of their insulating qualities. But the most important characteristic is that water will not stay with the fibers. So the bag can be wrung out and more easily dried. The main difference between the Dupont products and the others is that the Fiberfil II and Hollofil II are short, loose fibers while the PolarGuard and Thinsulate are in long fiber mats—a difference of little concern to campers.

The synthetic-fiber bags are more uniform than down bags in

filler. Therefore the quality of a synthetic-fiber bag can be pretty well determined by an inspection of the sewing, design, zipper, and other visible features. It is difficult to determine much about the filler in a down bag unless you're dealing with a very reputable company. Some down bags I've seen appear to have an inordinately large proportion of feathers, and feathers aren't down.

Shape and size of any sleeping bag are important considerations. So is stitching. The poorest bags are quilted, that is, sewn straight through. Good bags are illustrated in the maker's catalogues, showing how the fill is distributed in tubes, boxes, or wedges without any thin spots where the thread goes through. Some makers list the weight of the fill, such as "3-pound" or "2½ pound." Recently, more of them began listing the fill and total weight of the bag, which gives the camper a better picture. Fill weight indicates warmth. Total weight is what goes into the packsack.

Length can be a fooler. A guy who is six feet tall will be scrootched up like a hibernating groundhog in a six-foot bag. Rule of thumb calls for a bag 13 inches longer than the person's height. Some makers, like North Face, list recommended lengths for various heights of people.

Important as it is, the bag needs a mattress for proper use. A new idea in a combination air-and-foam mat called the Therm-A-Rest is being marketed by Cascade Designs, Inc., 4000 1st Ave., S., Seattle, Wash. 98134. Weighing just 1½ pounds, it unrolls from a 4″ × 21″ package to a 20″ × 47″ × 1½″ mat that self-inflates. Regular air mats are still popular and comfortable in mild weather if properly inflated. Campers with air mats should carry along small patching kits.

Foam mats offer better insulation, will not go flat, but are usually a little bulkier. The two types of commonly used foam are urethane open cell, 1 in. or 1½ in. thick; polyethylene foam closed cell, ⅜-inch thick. Closed cell, such as Ensolite, offers more ground insulation but is not as soft as urethane. For length, most people do not need a pad longer than the torso. A pad 42 to 48 inches long and 20 to 24 inches wide will handle anything except extreme cold. Pads come with or without covers. Beware of nylon covers, especially with a nylon bag. The camper with nylon-on-nylon may wake up to find he has tobogganed out of the tent.

We use the stuff bags from the sleeping bags for pillows, stuffing them with clothes and towels.

For light inside a tent, we use a thick plumber's candle stuck to a flat rock or the bottom side of a cook pot. We prop the metal mirror from the toilet kit to reflect more light. Some campers prefer a folding "candle lantern." We save our flashlight for outdoor emergency use. Gas or kerosene pressure lanterns are useful in a hunting or fishing base camp, but we could never see hauling a lantern and fuel on a canoe cruise.

So far, this whole exercise has been with two or more people and tents. The solo canoeist has a choice of a small nylon tent or going it with a tarp. I have used the tarp successfully by slinging it over the canoe, one end of which is propped up on a log or tree fork. A mosquito bar (GI surplus) is tied between the front and back thwarts (it usually just fits) and the bottom is against the ground. The tarp is guyed out over the top, using the canoe as a ridgepole. With an Ensolite pad and sleeping bag, the arrangement is fairly comfortable—barring prolonged rain. But then, I am not much of a loner. If I have my druthers, I go with somebody, share a bigger load, and live more comfortably.

After every trip, no matter how dry the weather, tent and bags are aired out (washed first if necessary), and checked for rips. Frayed ropes are replaced, mosquito netting is patched, and everything is made ready for the next trip.

Mildew is the bane of all fabric camping gear. Though nylon does not easily rot, the stitching might. And certainly any tent or bag stored damp will acquire a peculiar odor. The outfitters say, "Shake 'em out, wash 'em out, dry 'em out, and roll 'em up."

Chapter 9

Chow Down

Ask a hundred canoeists what the main hazards of a canoe trip are and the list will feature wind, rain, rapids, or insects, but seldom the greatest threat of all: the activity that takes place in the cook kit. Almost any flat-water traveler can withstand howling winds, an occasional chilly spill, and hosts of gnawing creatures browsing on his dermis. But let him face a couple of meals that come off like recycled sheep mash and the trip goes up for grabs.

If more than two people are in the party, arbitration may reduce premeditated murder to simple verbal abuse. But there is really no need for any culinary confrontation, not with the variety of tasty, nutritious, lightweight, easy-to-prepare trail foods available. Anyone who can read the instructions on the package can turn out a first-class meal in 30 minutes. The trail-food revolution has spawned a whole industry featuring names like Rich-Moor, Dry-Lite, Mountain House, Tea Kettle, Seidel, Bernard's, Chuck Wagon, Gumperts, and Canada Freeze Dry. And of course the big food companies supply supermarket shelves with numerous packaged items that readily adapt to packsack use.

The current generation of young campers has landed in this tasty trail-food paradise without having passed through the purgatory of the old food wanigan loaded with such staples as beans, bacon, flour, and prunes, supplemented by 80 pounds of canned everything, 90 percent of which was water. It was not age that made the old packers gnarled and stooped. They were simply crushed by the food packs.

Just a quick peek at the current list of available packaged items reveals omelets, blueberry pancake mix, bacon-flavored scrambled eggs, creamed chicken or tuna with noodles, beef Stroganoff, shrimp creole, spaghetti and meatballs, coffee cake, chop suey, lasagna, turkey Tetrazzini, cheese Romanoff, chicken salad, fruit cobbler, apple compote, pineapple cheese cake, gelatin fruit salad, lemon pie, banana cream pie, and on and on.

There are dozens of high-energy dishes that require no more than the addition of hot water. Freeze-dried steaks or beef patties come out of the package looking like pressed cardboard. Dunked in water, they puff up and emerge like fresh products from the butcher's block. A few ounces of confetti dumped out of a plastic bag converts to carrots, peas, green beans, sweet corn, or bell peppers. And soon to come along will be individual main meals, sealed in foil, that need only to be heated and eaten.

There may be some hoary-headed old bush cooks who sneer at meals from packets. But history will probably remember these lard-stained senior citizens along with stagecoach drivers and buffalo hunters. Not only can today's canoe chef turn out tastier, better-balanced fare, but he has little waste and little spoilage. With better-preserved, better-packaged foods, there has been a corresponding decrease in the incidence of intestinal disorders. From the standpoint of palate and stomach, these are the good old days of outdoor cookery.

None of this is intended to disparage experience with spoon and spatula. On the contrary. Even though a novice cook can turn out a fine meal with today's ingredients, the veteran can create a gourmet spread. Knowledge of seasonings, timing, and fresh additions from waters and woodlands are bits of cook-fire magic that come only with practice.

But first, forsooth, you must have a kitchen wherein to cook. Most cooks seek out a fairly open spot, at least partially sheltered from the wind, and containing a slab of ledge or area of mineral soil where a small fireplace may be erected or the stove seated. For cooking, a small, low fire offers fingertip control. Or, as my friend Stanley Owl likes to say: "Build small fire, stand close. Build big fire, stand far away."

The grate may be adjusted horizontally by using a pan full of water as a level and shimming the low sides of the grate with shards of rock. If wind becomes a problem after the fireplace is up, a few large, flat stones set on edge and leaning in from the windward side will shelter the flames.

If there is a hint of rain in the air, the kitchen fly can be slung and guyed out to cover the working and eating area. In no instance except in extreme weather or where insect hordes are unbearable is food taken inside the tent to eat. The attraction to Mother Nature's little woodland friends is too great a risk.

With the kitchen in place, the table is brought up from the lakeshore. Flat-bottom canoes make the best tables, but any canoe will work. Horizontal deadfall log supports are set so the canoe will rest upside down on its gunwales. Plates, cups, pots, utensils, water, and food items for that meal may be set thereon. Where open fires are permitted or preferred, ample wood is stacked in readiness. Or the camp stove is fueled up, leveled, and lit. Lightweight, single-burner imports such as Optimus, Primus, Phoebus, or Svea are all excellent for small parties. Two-burner Colemans are standard for bigger groups, although they are much heavier and bulkier. We use a 111-B Optimus because it heats quickly and has a pressure pump that allows the unit to function during winter camping trips at 30 and 40 below. Of course there are not many canoeists out fooling around in that weather. We aren't paddling then, we are skiing. Recently we tested the new single-burner Coleman Peak I and found them excellent unless filled more than two-thirds full when they tend to leak gas. They are light and sell for approximately one-half the price of the Optimus.

Every cook has his equipment preferences. For four or more people we use a Mirro kit, the one with the 12-inch aluminum frying pan lid, which is not much good for frying but makes a fine mixing dish. We take a cast-aluminum Shore-Barb griddle for

Single Burner Cook Stove

general frying and also an aluminum Benn-Don Dutch oven, which is superb for baking. Some people like a reflector oven, and this rig bakes well. We don't use one because we bake in the Dutch oven or frying pan. Frying pan? Yep. I'll explain a little later.

When just two of us go, we take a set of three nesting pots, each with a lid and a folding wire handle. We also take a folding fabric bucket for water. Some guides use steel frying pans, excellent for cooking and light in weight.

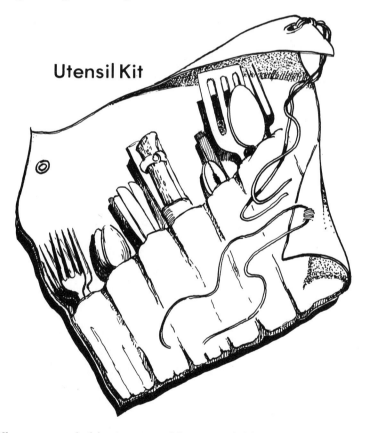

Utensil Kit

Whatever cook kit you use, it's a good idea to either buy or make a bag with a drawstring to cover it. The bag will keep the kit separated from sleeping bags and other gear in a packsack. Also, the grate and griddle should be in a cloth bag to prevent any soot from getting on the pack and other equipment. A roll-up cloth pouch, slotted to hold knives, forks, spoons, and cooking tools, is handy. We include a pair of pliers, fillet knife in a sheath, spatula, long-handled fork, and a big spoon. A small, fine, flat file or steel fits in the utensil bag and is used for sharpening. A file will run about one buck, a good steel from $5 to $8. A stone is preferred by some campers. For a real sharpening job we use a Razor-Edge Systems kit before the trip. This is the best sharpening outfit we have ever seen and is made by John Juranitch at P.O. Box 604, Ely, Minn. 55731.

We carry two fire starters in the cook pack: the GI-type tablets in foil which are kept for emergency wet conditions, and a roll of wax paper for general use. A small piece of wax paper bunched up, will normally start kindling quickly. On this starter can be laid the wood slivers, dry twigs, weed stalks, pine needles, and bark strips to kindle bigger pieces. Dry birchbark from downed and dead trees is a pitch-loaded starter; however, no thoughtful camper any longer pulls loose bark from the outside of live birch trees.

A moderate stack of "squaw wood," from the size of a pencil to thumb-thick and about 10 inches long, will provide a flame about as easily regulated as the gas range at home. Prior to any food preparation, wash your hands thoroughly with soap. In the Minnesota Guide School where I taught for several years, student guides were instructed to make a show of washing their hands before preparing a meal as a method of impressing on their clients the need for clean camp habits. The hand-washing exercise can be integrated with the pot-soaping ceremony, a vital procedure when you're cooking on open fires. A small bit of liquid soap spread evenly with the fingers or paper towel over the *outside* of each cook pot will create a thin film upon which all smoky soot will collect, and which can be easily washed off later in hot water. Extreme care must be taken to keep any stray flicks of soap from getting *inside* any pot where food will be prepared. Even a small amount of soap in food can react like a double-barreled laxative.

Before the first match is struck, all food preparation that can be accomplished in advance is attended to in order to save time and fuel. In the morning, this includes preparing orange or grapefruit drink. Two items we usually have going first are the coffee pot and a pail of water, which will be used for washing dishes. Coffee is brewed (not boiled) by putting one heaping tablespoon in cold water for each four cups, plus a little extra tossed in "for the cook." While other food preparations are underway, the coffee pot is on the flame. When the first bubbles start coming up the spout, the pot is set to the side where it will stay hot and the grounds will settle. Some people add eggs, egg shells, and various other things to make the grounds settle. But *our* grounds settle just fine when we take the pot off the direct flame.

If there is a diversity of beverage drinkers, or if we are using a gas stove, the water is simply heated to the boiling point, then set aside to be added as wished to cups with instant coffee, tea, chocolate, or bouillon. In cold weather we often make up cups of hot Tang, which are superb frost dispellers.

Now for the main meal. The trick of putting together any streamside banquet is to get everything to come out at the same time. Nobody likes to sit around watching the fish get cold while waiting for the potatoes to cook. Everything takes a certain time to get "done." It is up to the cook to schedule his activity so the longest-cooking items are on first. Fortunately, the packeted trail foods and premixed items from the grocer's shelves have cooking times printed on the outside of the bag or box. Anyone who can tell time can figure out what goes first. With a little experience, sequences get memorized, and the cook procedes almost automatically.

For a large group, it may not be possible to have everything on the fire at once. Or even with two people, some items can be cooked and kept warm at the side. Breakfast bacon, for instance, comes off the griddle early and winds up draining on a bit of paper towel inside a tin that is placed to reflect the fire's heat. The bacon stays crisp and warm while the eggs or pancakes steam on the griddle.

Potatoes may be cooked ahead and set at the edge of the fire. Macaroni, rice, spaghetti, and noodle dishes are in this same category. Covered aluminum pots will absorb heat even some distance from the fire and keep the contents hot. All cooks know, or should know, that aluminum can quickly get too hot. People who have cursed while scouring black off the *outside* of an aluminum pot will need a whole new set of words to get the black off the *inside* of a pot.

Another trick that works well in controlling heat while tending several pots at once is the judicious use of a tablespoon or two of water to dampen the flames slightly.

In those hallowed days of yore, when food items were bought by the pound, grub lists were a great source of speculation and even entertainment, sometimes consuming more time than the trips themselves. Making a menu today is relatively simple, although care must be taken on longer safaris to pay close attention to nutrition. On a short ten-day trip, we might split up breakfasts among eggs, cereal (cooked), coffee cake, stewed fruit, pancakes, with bacon as a side dish (precooked when we can get it), coffee, Tang, and chocolate. Lunches are built around a cold juice drink, sausage, cheese, dehydrated cheese packets, peanut butter, jam, packaged tuna or chicken salad. We eat this with Rye Krisp, crackers, Hudson Bay Bread or bannock.

We make what we call "Bout Bannock" which can be baked ahead of time or prepackaged dry and baked on the trail. There are dozens of good outdoor cookbooks, so we will not try to insert a mess of recipes here, but Bout Bannock we make like this: 'bout three cups of flour, 'bout a tablespoon of baking powder, a little sugar, 'bout a half teaspoon salt, 'bout a double handful of raisins or cut-up dried fruit, and a half cup dry milk stirred well together. When ready to bake, add 2 tablespoons of cooking oil, stir, and 'bout a cup of water, slowly kneading the dough until it turns into a rubbery ball. Dust a little flour on the canoe "table" and punch that rubber dough into a flat disk the same size as the bottom of the frying pan. Grease the pan good, drop in the dough, and let the pan sit on the fire until the dough browns on the bottom. Take the pan off, prop it up facing the fire, 'bout a foot away, and bake the top until it just gets brown. It is ready to eat on the spot or can be stowed away for a day or two.

Hudson Bay Bread is really a huge cookie that will make a full lunch if it's spread with peanut butter or jam. Guide Bud Dickson's wife Sandy makes this food up for their Ontario outfitting business thus: mix 2 cups margarine, 2 cups sugar, ⅓ cup corn syrup, 1⅜ cup honey, 9 cups dry oatmeal, 1 cup coconut. Roll it out flat on a greased cookie tin and bake for about 25 minutes at 350 degrees. Cut into 4-inch squares and wrap in foil. This Hudson Bay Bread will last for more than three weeks on the trail.

We seldom take fresh meat along on any trip, because tons of it are swimming under the canoe. We figure fish for supper at least every other day, sometimes more. We fry 'em, poach 'em in milk, bake 'em, and make fish chowder out of 'em. One of the most common and most easily caught species of fish in the north is the pike, seemingly all teeth and appetite. Some people ignore this source of protein because of the "Y" bones along the lateral line. Removing these is a snap, and here is how to do it: fillet the pike (skin off), and cut the fillet crosswise into 3-inch chunks. The tailpiece will have no Y bones. On the other pieces, feel along the insides above where the ribs were. You can detect the two lines of bones, even see them with a little practice. This is the top of the Y, the tail of the Y curves below and toward the dorsal. Insert your knife outside the top of the Y, slice down, and curve toward the dorsal. The tail of the bones will be clearly seen in a white row. Now slice behind the other side of the Y, down and curving toward the dorsal, and this process will remove the bones with a small piece of meat. Toss this away. The rest is boneless. When all the pieces are boned out, the remaining meat is some of the finest available anywhere.

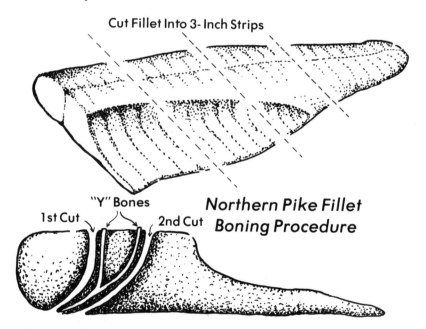

Cut Fillet Into 3- Inch Strips

"Y" Bones

1st Cut   2nd Cut

Northern Pike Fillet Boning Procedure

Incidentally, the proper disposal of fish entrails and bones is a source of debate. Some fishermen say bury 'em in the woods, some say leave 'em on the shore for seagulls. In either case, entrails and bones should be left a good distance from camp so they do not attract bears.

In season, berries make a welcome addition to the menu. Some people time their trips to coincide with the northern blueberry season in July and early August. Some good books describe edible plants and mushrooms for the outdoorsman who wants to spice up his menu. Mushrooms, of course, have little food value, but they add taste to any meal. However, you must know which mushrooms are edible. There's no room for guesswork here. The *Mushroom Hunters Guide* by Alexander H. Smith is one we have used for many years.

Pushing a paddle burns up a lot of calories. The canoeist, like the backpacker who stops every hour or so for liquid intake and some high-energy "munchies," will usually operate better with frequent stops, a drink of water, and a handful or two of "gorp"—nuts, candy, wheat germ, raisins—from a pocket bag, or some homemade granola. At least it will keep a lid on the appetite until suppertime, when the fires of hunger can be more adequately quenched.

Chapter 10

Fishing from a Canoe

In the first chapter of Genesis it is recorded that when the Lord created the earth, He initially produced a sphere entirely covered with water (Gen. 1:2). A few verses beyond, He said, "Let the waters bring forth swarms of living creatures," thus engaging in the world's first fish-stocking project prior to the creation of any other living species. Now, no matter how weak and backsliding the human animal may be, those sinners among us who comprise the international congregation of anglers have at least strictly adhered to our Lord's original concept: The fish come first. And we will go any distance, expend any amount, endure any hardship to practice our faith.

Historically, when the first Asiatic nomads crossed the Bering land bridge, edged down into the timber-rimmed lake country, and began building their bark craft, it did not take them long to combine canoe and handline for harvesting pike and trout. However, the concept of the fishing rod and angling for sport was brought to the continent by the starched and upright English colonists among whom were sprinkled a few contemporaries of Izaak Walton, men who quickly perceived the advantage of casting a line from light, portable craft. Included were some of my forebears from Somersetshire who held the opinion, so it is rumored, that had those unfortunate women of Salem learned the art of tying a good Coachman, the menfolk would never have allowed them to be broiled for witchcraft. This is speculation, of course, but there are records of New England's sporting folk using birchbark canoes to reach remote waters long before the first British musket went off at Breed's Hill.

As the frontier was pushed back, the use of lightweight, maneuverable boats to reach the backcountry increased with each succeeding generation of anglers. Thus, anywhere gamefish are found in North America today, there are men with canoes seeking them out.

Beyond the affliction of sport fishing, to which many of us are addicted, is a secondary reason that angling is an important aspect of canoe camping: an inexhaustible supply of fresh meat is available under the hull of the boat, a supply that need not be packed or portaged. All that is required is a small tackle kit and a basic knowledge of the advantages and limitations of the craft as applied to the pursuit.

Bait-casting, spin-casting, and fly-casting tackle all handle well from a canoe. Takedown pack rods that fit into a packsack are handy, although regular two- or three-piece outfits with aluminum or plastic cases work about as well, the cases lashed to the thwarts for traveling.

Canoe Trip Tackle

Single Hook Lures

Experienced canoe anglers carry their terminal tackle in small lure boxes that fit in the pockets of their jackets or fishing vests. Single-hook lures such as jigs are preferred, or lures with only one treble hook. Plugs with multiple gang hooks are dangerous within the limited legroom of a canoe when brought aboard decorating the jaw of a thrashing fish. It is nearly impossible to get snagged on a single hook, and one treble hook may generally be avoided. Some wilderness anglers even replace trebles on spinners and spoons with single hooks.

The risk of getting a hook slammed into the epidermis is greater in 15-foot or shorter canoes where the bowman is within closer reach on his backcast. Guides minimize this problem by the way they position the canoe in regard to the bowman's casting arm. That is, if the bowman is right-handed, then the canoe is moved along the left shore so that his backcasts and forward casts travel across the bow, out of harm's way.

But hooks are only one problem. It would be a good bet, at 2 to 1 odds, that more canoeists swamp while fishing than while paddling. When underway, both canoeists are alert to the movements of each other, each has a paddle in hand to compensate for any assault on the law of gravity. In a fishing situation, only the stern paddler has a comprehensive picture of what transpires, and his attention may be distracted momentarily when the bowman makes an erratic move.

Professional canoe guides, exposed day in and day out to a variety of fishermen, develop keen dexterity with the paddle brace to offset over-eager clients. Even worse is the sloucher, who insists on sitting off center. This maneuver keeps his concerned partner hanging out the opposite side in a precarious, spine-twisting balance. It is pure pleasure to fish with a partner who knows how to keep his body planted dead center and moves only his arms and feet.

In most instances, it is safest for the stern man to handle the landing net. Again, he has the best overall picture of the situation and can more easily maintain balance while the fish is led into the mesh. He has more legroom to handle the fish while unhooking it. He is also in a better position to handle the stringer. A stringer hanging from the bow area will drag in the water and continually pull the canoe toward one side, making it difficult to paddle. A stringer of fish off the stern won't help the canoe move faster, but at least the craft tends to ride straight.

Some fishermen prefer a canvas glove for landing fish, rather than a net. Certainly a glove is less bulky and is easily carried in a pocket. We sometimes carry a small folding net that will fit inside the pack, or a short floating net that can be tucked up under the flap. When fishing, the stern man keeps the net stowed amidships against the left gunwale, handle resting atop the stern thwart. His paddle leans against the right gunwale, grip resting on the rear thwart. The bowman stows his paddle behind the seat, blade against the gunwale and handle on the front thwart or on the seat brace. When one angler hooks a big fish, his partner reels in and uses his paddle to keep the canoe from drifting into weeds or snags.

In the event an exceptionally large trophy is hooked, it may be best not to bring it into the canoe at all. One late-fall evening, when the slanting sun ignited the shoreline maples in splashes of orange flame, Lil and I were trolling little No. 1 Mepps spinners for walleyes on nearby Ensign Lake. We had nearly assembled the necessary ingredients for supper when a big shark of a northern pike cracked my lure and proceeded to blaze a trail through two acres of underwater vegetation. Patiently, Lil followed with her paddle while I carefully extracted my six-pound monofilament from the cabbage patch. After some 20 minutes of this, the big fish broke into the open and surfaced, all four feet of him. Lil, backpaddling to a gravel bar, beached the canoe, picked up a stout birch cudgel, and stalked the trophy while I eased him into the shallows. With one swift stroke, Lil terminated his career, and it was a simple matter to slide those 25 pounds of inert pike steak up the shore. If we had been in a remote situation where we could not have used the meat, we would have simply cut the light line, freeing the fish unharmed.

When handling toothy critters such as pike and walleyes, you need a pair of long-nosed pliers with built-in side cutters. Some veteran anglers carry their pliers in a leather sheath on their hip in place of a big knife. Besides removing hooks from fish, these pliers are also handy for removing hooks from people, the plier portion used to force the hook point on through the skin and the side cutters to clip off the barb so the hook can be backed out. Another handy tool is a small, chromed clipper, used to trim monofilament knots as well as fingernails.

Thus far I've discussed spin casting and bait casting, but not fly casting. The use of a fly rod in a canoe requires special considerations. For one, the angle of the canoe to the target area must be continually adjusted to keep the long backcast from caressing the stern man's earlobe. In most situations, it works best for one man to cast while the other handles the craft, the anglers occasionally beaching the craft to change positions.

Some flycasters prefer to work standing up. Once upon a time I fished with a superb fly rodder named Roy Nord, who had learned his skill in Michigan's Upper Penninsula. Roy cast standing in the bow of my 18-foot canvas Guide Model, his left foot slightly forward, his right leg braced against the wicker seat. So impeccable was his casting skill and so perfect his balance, the canoe never wavered. On the other hand, this account should not be taken as a testimony for stand-up canoe fishing. Not all canoes have that wide, initial stability. And not all anglers are that skilled.

Trolling is an easy and productive method of canoe angling. Often we troll the last mile or so to the evening campsite, bow and stern fishermen with lines opposite the paddle side. That is, if the stern paddler is paddling right, his line is out the left, the bowman the opposite. The rod butt can be anchored under the paddle-side knee so that a strike doesn't take the outfit overboard.

An effective one-man method of trolling jigs is to hold the rod and paddle together, butt end of the rod in the lower hand, middle section of the rod in the upper hand. With each stroke, you whip the lure erratically forward. This technique takes some getting used to, but it's murder on walleyes and lake trout.

Three people can fish from one canoe, the odd person being located between the middle and stern thwarts. Old Town, Grumman, Chestnut, and several other manufacturers make lightweight middle seats. Guides around our part of the country use an empty 24-bottle wooden Coke box with a boat-cushion seat and a cushion against the stern thwart for a backrest. With the bow and middle man fishing, usually the stern man simply handles the paddle.

One frequently encountered problem with canoe fishing is wind. It blows, sometimes all day. Quite often the best fishing is alongshore where the waves are breaking in. An anchor is a handy item in this situation, either a folding-fin metal hook or simply a nylon mesh bag filled with rocks. The bag is light and takes up no room in a pack. A good-sized rock tied four ways will work, too. A coil of cheap cotton rope makes a good occasional anchor line.

Sometimes, even in remote areas, fish do not go exactly wild over lures. Occasionally a pork strip added to a jig or spoon will do the job. Sometimes live bait works best. Where legal, canoeists may pack in six feet of minnow net, to seine shiners or chubs in the shallows. Frogs are an excellent north-country bait, even those little gray peepers. Frogs need not be captured alive. Indeed, they are a better bait dead, as long as they are fresh. They can be quickly harvested in weedy shallows with a three-foot stick and kept in a wet sock. Gullet, the pink V-shaped piece of meat from a walleye's underjaw, makes an excellent bait. So are the grey leeches that inhabit riffles. The reddish green bloodsucker leech is worthless as bait.

One recurring problem with wilderness trips is not in catching fish, but in catching far more fish than can be eaten. If the main meal of the day is fish, a decision should be made early on how many are necessary and who in the group should be designated the "meat hunters." A good rule of the fin-scarred thumb is to string two pounds of fish "on the hoof" for each person and release the rest unharmed.

In the early spring, when some snow still survives in the shade, fish can be kept in a snowbank. Another method of keeping fish overnight is to put a 50-foot nylon line extension on the stringer, tie a rock to it, and sink the live fish out in deep, cold water away from shore. The shore end of the line is tied to a tree.

If you intend to pack out a trophy to a taxidermist, use the long line to keep the fish alive as long as possible, up to the last day. To pack a dead fish out, remove the gills, wrap the fish in a wet T-shirt to protect the scales and keep the fins pliant. Cushion the trophy in the packsack with loose, damp moss. When a point is reached where freezer service is available, pack the trophy between two pieces of cardboard and tape it in place so nothing will hit the brittle fins. An excellent reference is Edward C. Migdalski's *How To Make Fish Mounts,* published by The Ronald Press, 79 Madison Avenue, New York, N.Y. 10016.

A good day's fishing means considerable blood and fish juice on the inside bottom of the canoe. It is good practice to slosh a dozen buckets of water around the inside of the craft and set it upside down to drain. This practice means a clean, odorless, insect-free canoe in the morning.

Chapter 11

Fly-in, Canoe-out Trips

Float planes have come a long way since 1911, when the first U.S. pontoon-equipped crate was lifted off the water by a 32-year-old flier named Glen Curtiss. From that flight evolved a new avenue of air travel that opened thousands of square miles of wilderness to the recreational canoeist and at the same time offered government cartographers a means of photographing and charting remote areas that has provided us with our current, accurate maps.

The first real "bush pilots" were unemployed World War I combat fliers who would try anything with wings and a motor. Careers were often brief in the 1920s, but by 1930 technology had supplied reliable Curtiss Robins, Fairchilds, and at least one Ford Tri-Motor on floats (with two of the engines pulled to save weight) that were regularly flying people and freight into the backcountry. From these descended the current crop of dependable Cessnas, Otters, Beavers, and Twin Beechcrafts on pontoons. Considering distances flown and costs of equipment, fuel, and insurance, float-plane fees are one of the few genuine bargains left in the world. Maybe that's why nobody ever runs into a rich bush pilot.

I don't mean to imply that flying is cheaper than driving a car. Far from it. Current costs, differing from one carrier to another, run several dollars per mile depending on the type of aircraft. A Twin Beech with a cargo door will handle two canoes inside plus four men, gear, and enough food for a month. A 200-mile flight would currently (1983) run about $560 or $140 each. Two men, gear, and food, with a canoe strapped to the struts of a Beaver, would pay $380 for the same flight, or $190 each. A Beaver is the smallest plane with passengers that the law allows a canoe to be strapped on the outside of.

If your party has six paddlers, a big Otter will handle passengers, food, gear, two canoes inside and one lashed outside for $660 over a 200-mile route which tallies out at $110 a person. When you figure 200 air miles may cover from 500 to 800 canoe miles, the cost is well justified.

Contact with float-plane operators can be made through U.S. and Canadian outdoor magazines, listings in tourist-association folders, and in government travel-department directories. Representatives of such outfits appear at the various U.S. and Canadian sport shows. Bush pilots are generally quite knowledgeable about their areas of operation and will discuss details of canoe routes, campsites, fishing, hunting, weather, and the feasibility of a proposed trip.

One of the most popular and least costly combinations is a fly-in and canoe-back setup, which requires only a one-way air fare and no problems about scheduling pickup time. Another well-used system is to drive a car to a jump-off point, paddle to a prearranged pickup spot and fly back to your car. When a pickup is arranged for a remote spot, it must be kept in mind that weather can delay aircraft and can also delay the canoeist. If the plane is on schedule but the paddlers aren't, the flight must be paid for anyway. No bush pilot is going to tie up his aircraft for more than a few hours because of tardy campers.

It is good practice to schedule the pickup at a settlement, trading post, ranger station, lodge, or some point of human habitation where contact can be made with the "outside" in the event of a foul-up. It is also good practice to allow at least one extra day in excess of anticipated travel time as a pad against delay. Obviously, this scheduling requires the canoeists to have an accurate idea of their own ability—miles per day they normally paddle—as applied to the waterways they will be traveling. Consideration must be given where big lakes and wind can cause delays. And don't forget meandering waters and swamps where map and compass work may be involved. Rapids and waterfalls with accompanying portages will raise hob with time schedules, particularly in remote areas where trails may be poorly defined or simply nonexistent. Unless you know the country intimately, an average of 10 to 15 miles of paddling per day may be realistic. With a motor, the distance may jump to 25 or 30, or it may not be any faster at all, depending on water depth and the number of portages involved. But the unexpected should be anticipated.

Dan Litchfield and Mark Van Tassel, two of our Ely, Minnesota, neighbors, made a 1,130-mile, 73-day tour up into the Athabasca country in 1976, an area of big lakes and some canoe-eating white water. A few days before the end of their trip they came upon a gaunt, tattered survivor of an accident that had occurred in a rapids on the Cochrane River 18 days earlier. The man had lost his companion, canoe, and outfit. Alone, he was following the stream course, eating whatever he could scrounge up. Dan and Mark took the man aboard, paddled to a cabin several miles downstream, and dropped him off with most of their food.

With the lightened canoe, they paddled almost continually until they reached a village where an available float plane was dispatched to pick up the survivor. The incident crimped our neighbors' food supply and terminated their trip, but nobody ever passes up a fellow camper in trouble.

An emergency can throw a flight schedule out of whack. In the event of an injury to someone in the bush or a forest fire, any available bush pilots may be sent to that emergency first. Scheduled flights or pickups would then be "bumped" back. Which is another good reason for flying in and canoeing back out.

All details of the trip must be anchored long before the flight date. Most float-plane operators are very busy in the summer and trips are handled on a first-come, first-served basis. It is easy in January to book a flight for, let's say, 8 A.M. on June 15. But the canoeist who makes a last-minute reservation or simply drives into the seaplane base expecting to fly out immediately may be in for an exasperating wait.

Flight date, time, and drop-off point must be nailed down as far in advance as possible with a cash deposit. Also, it is well to check on allowed weights and canoe sizes. Some aircraft cannot handle canoes longer than 17 feet. Figuring loads, a Beaver will haul about 1,300 pounds total, a Beech will take 1,700, and an Otter will go about 2,300 pounds. People who regularly fly commercial airlines know that extra baggage weight simply means an additional charge, but not so with the float planes. Additional weight means you can't get off the water, so the pilot must throw equipment out.

Another important weight consideration should be made clear: when a canoe is lashed to the outside of a plane, the "drag" in the air is equal to three times the weight of the canoe. So if you're figuring your flight weight for a Beaver and your canoe is 75 pounds, compute this as 225 pounds against your total allowable load. Canoes carried inside, such as in a Twin Beech, are computed at the regular weight.

Fly-in canoe trips involving outboard motors are becoming increasingly involved in red tape. The problem lies with government regulations on flying cans of gasoline along with passengers. If you plan to use an outboard, discuss the gas situation fully with the float-plane operator well in advance. It is not much fun paddling a square-stern canoe over a wilderness route.

All paperwork, licenses, permits, and customs clearances must be considered in advance. If the flight originates in the U.S., either with an American carrier or a Canadian pickup, cash or traveler's checks must be sufficient to cover customs charges, fishing licenses, and any permits needed. Canadian Customs officers and Canadian rangers do not accept personal checks. All licenses and permits must be bought in advance of any flight originating in Canada.

One of the dumbest tricks that can trip up U.S. canoeists is getting flown to a remote area, discovering they forgot to get fishing licenses, and then assuming that since they are so far out in the bush, no one will know anyway. Don't bet on it. Provincial departments of natural resources are staffed with mobile, highly trained personnel that are on constant patrol. A good amount of this is done from the air, and flying conservation officers with field glasses can spot a canoe on the water just as easily as the canoeists can spot the plane in the air. Canadian officers do not appreciate U.S. citizens trying to slip something over, and the results can be disastrous. In the U.S., a fisherman caught without a license is usually haled before a judge and fined $25 or so. In Canada, a fish or game violation can result in a much stiffer fine, confiscation of all equipment involved, including canoe and camping outfit, and an abrupt termination of the trip. Looked at from any angle, it is a darn poor trade. Furthermore, it is embarrassing to the float-plane operator, and he won't be one bit sympathetic.

Canoeists who run a checklist on their equipment should rerun that list when boarding a plane. Once you're airborne, there's no easy way to acquire that forgotten map or sleeping bag. Canadian government regulations on life jackets are very strict. A good number of fly-in canoe trips have ended at a ranger station when it was discovered that four canoeists had only three personal floatation devices.

Float planes provide the fastest method of getting around big areas of the northern bush, in some instances the only way. But with all of their facility and relatively accident-free operation, the weather factor is still a headache. Bush pilots are extremely tough, hardy, and iron-nerved. Lil and I have flown in tough situations with them, from threading our way through Quebec's Laurentians in a May snowstorm to being forced down in a blinding fog on a Minnesota pothole lake. We have come in with enough ice on the wings to surface a hockey rink and have groped through the top of a storm-shrouded Ontario spruce forest with a moose carcass for a seat. On the other hand, we have "sat out" some weather that didn't seem nearly as bad. But if the pilot didn't want to fly, we didn't either. In bush pilot Pat Magies's operations shack is this motto: "There are old pilots and there are bold pilots, but there are no old, bold pilots."

Chapter 12

Hunting by Canoe

A raw northwest wind moaned through the fir tops, whipped skeins of snow across the black surface of Gun Lake, and rattled the taut nylon tarp that sheltered our small cook stove. Doc Spangler squinted into the wind, hands wrapped around a steaming cup of coffee, head turned to one side, listening. "There's some mallards movin' out there," he said.

Lil and I stepped to the edge of the tarp. Distinct from the wind, we detected the rhythmic beat of feathered pinions in the predawn darkness, coupled with the faint "cutta-cutta-cut" gabble of greenheads moving toward a feeding area. Doc grinned, finished off his coffee, and administered a dozen or so pumps to the hissing Coleman lantern. On one burner of the gas stove, the dented coffee pot steamed industriously. On the other, eggs and thick slabs of bacon were being rendered into breakfast. "The trouble with a trip like this," said Doc, surveying the cozy scene, "is that it has to end sometime."

We were a few miles from the Minnesota-Ontario border in an area frequented by summer canoeists, but in October we hadn't seen another soul all week. This is no local phenomenon. Once September's golden days are gone, the canoe trails of the north are deserted except for the occasional hunter or trapper. You can expect a few weather hazards, but you'll also enjoy a lot of pluses. First is a complete absence of the little beggars that fly and bite, eliminating your need for protecting creams, liquids, or nets. Airborne microspores no longer torment the respiratory tracts of the allergic. Newly washed spruce and pine contrast with the bright golden birch and aspen, punctuated here and there by exclamation points of red maple. At dawn, wraiths of blue mist, like ghosts of ancient Ojibwa warriors, dance along the still waters. On clear nights, as frost is brushed in white strokes on rock, stump, and lichen, the stars crowd down for a closer look at the silent forest. It is a time when the outdoors cleanses itself, when migratory creatures wing toward warmer climates, and the resident species thicken their coats for the freeze-up. It's also a time for the human animal to renew mind and soul. Which was why we were up on Gun Lake.

Doc and I had grown up on the same street in Illinois, gone to the same schools, hunted the same marshes and uplands, and fished and canoed the same rivers until our paths had parted. He went on to Northwestern University Dental School, served in Korea, and became a dentist for the Veterans' Administration. I, meantime, had a hitch with the Marines in World War II, married Lil, spawned two daughters, and put in 16 years covering outdoor sports for three different newspapers before migrating to northern Minnesota to become an outfitter and guide.

One day a letter arrived from Doc saying that he had grown old and tired as a tooth carpenter and felt perhaps he was due a respite from the pain of the world, a brief time to heft a spinning rod, sight down the rib of a shotgun, and maybe listen to the hunting cry of a timber-wolf pack instead of a roomful of people with sore jaws.

On the trail, it took about three days for that haunted, fluorescent-light look to vanish from Doc's eyes—three days of busting ruffled grouse out of the raspberry bushes, whipping jut-jawed smallmouth bass, and jumping greenhead drakes out of wild-rice patches. In three days he shed 30 years.

Our camp was pitched in a small, sandy clearing, sheltered on three sides by protecting trees and open to the south to absorb any available sunlight. Our steep-roofed "A" tent shed both rain and snow and zipped up at night like a cocoon. Our 14 x 16 nylon kitchen tarp was pitched taut over a smooth ridgepole from which hung the gas lantern. Two large flat rocks balanced the cook stove, and a pine log supplied seating. A line strung beneath the tarp accommodated wet jackets and pants for drying. The gas lantern was used inside the tent sparingly at bedtime for illumination and to eliminate the chill, but only sparingly because of possible carbon-monoxide buildup. The cook stove was never used inside the tent for the same reason, and because of fire hazard.

Along with our Ensolite pads and winter bags, we kept in the tent only those items that had to be available: flashlight, toilet paper, reading material, candles, extra sox and underwear, and a small whisk broom that we used to remove snow, leaves, and twigs.

On the ground at the edge of the tarp we cleared away a circle of leaves and needles where we could safely kindle a wood cook fire when weather permitted, a blaze that doubled as a clothes drier and body warmer on cold evenings. With the camp snugged down, we next considered how to make contact with the water-fowl, which we did with enough success to send Doc home with a packsackful of memories.

On any fall hunting trip, the problem of swamping in icy waters is not something to fret over, but it is certainly something to think about. Some north-country gunners acquire hunting jackets an extra size larger so that brightly colored PFDs can be hidden underneath, and some hunters spray-paint camouflage on their life jackets; but if their vests are as old and soiled as our Stearns models, there isn't enough bright orange left to spook even the most nervous winged migrant.

All canoeists are aware of water hazards, but not as many consider the equally real cold-weather threats of dehydration, overexertion, and fatigue. To keep these sneaky risks nullified, we nibble periodically on gorp and dried fruit, drink frequent half-cups of lake water, and use a hot pot of instant soup to bolster our noon sandwiches.

The mechanics of hunting waterfowl by canoe follows relatively simple rules. We pack in a dozen deflatable plastic mallards and a dozen bluebills, which can all be rolled up in one Duluth pack with enough room left for lunch. Mallard decoys will entice any of the puddleduck species we're apt to encounter, and the bluebills will toll ringbills, goldeneye, or buffleheads, as well as scaup. Wilderness waterfowl are usually not as sophisticated as the same birds encountered farther south after they have become more wary of boats, blinds, and decoys. But they do not come in with surrender flags unfurled, either. Usually we make a temporary blind from dead wood, brush, and grass. But we have, at times, packed in an old minnow seine, its floats and sinkers removed, to drape over sticks for camouflage.

The principal problem with wilderness waterfowl shooting is that other hunters are seldom around to keep the ducks moving, and the ducks have hundreds of lakes and rivers where they can raft up without your being aware. When decoy activity is zero, we engage in jump-shooting from the canoe, first tossing a coin for the bow seat. There may be some hunters who shoot double in a canoe, but I don't want somebody unloading a full charge of #6 shot past my ear while I am crouched in the bow. Furthermore, there is considerable effect from the recoil of a shot to the side. Simultaneous bow and stern shots on the same side can capsize a craft.

In tall rice or reeds, especially in a wind, it is sometimes possible to paddle quite close to ducks before they jump. In more open situations with scant cover, the canoe can be "snuck in" by the use of a small, one-handed ping-pong size paddle, a method used by natives in the far north. You kneel, body low, eyes just even with the gunwales. The canoe is angled downwind slightly to the side of the ducks so the single-handed paddling can be done out of view. Nothing moves except your wrist, the paddle, and the canoe, which seems to the ducks like some inanimate thing drifting down on them. The paddle handle is drilled and tied to a thwart with a piece of line so that when the time comes to shoot, you merely let go of your paddle and come up with your scatter-gun. To work this stalk successfully, you must take care to start directly upwind from the ducks lest you drift to one side out of range.

We draw our birds immediately after the hunt, while they are still warm. Regulations on keeping wings, head, and feet on gamebirds vary in different states and provinces and must be followed to the letter. In most fall weather, a drawn duck will cool quickly and will keep well for a week or more. If we are ending the trip shortly, we will also pluck the warm ducks. Feathers left on after the birds cool are harder to pluck, but the feathers prevent the birds from drying out. We use a plastic or cloth bag to haul the birds out when we break camp. If the weather is warm, though, we don't leave them in plastic, because they will deteriorate rapidly without circulating air.

In cold weather, ice will likely form on the craft and on the paddles. A pair of rubber gloves tucked into your duffle can be a finger-saver when you pick up decoys or downed birds. The canoe should be pulled up and turned over at night so that accumulated water will drain out and not turn to ice, and so falling sleet or snow doesn't pile up inside. Paddles placed in the shelter of the tarp will remain dry and ice-free.

Ice along the shore can create treacherous footing on rocks and

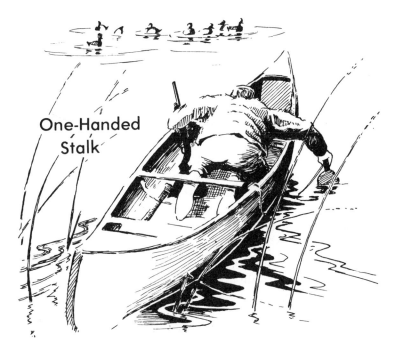

One-Handed
Stalk

logs. We load up with one person in the canoe, both hands free for balance, then pass in the equipment and guns before the other hunter comes aboard. Also, it is well to secure the canoe with a bowline when the shore is slippery.

One October, Lil and I were back in a small Ontario trout lake. We beached our craft, moved the duffle up the bank, and prepared to pitch camp. It was snowing slightly, and the shore was slick. With the last pack unloaded from it, the canoe simply slid out into the lake and started downwind alone. There was a sharp clutch in my gut when I saw the situation, but the options were few.

Peeling off my clothes, I hit that icy water, stroking toward the canoe even though most of my breath was stuck just below my Adam's apple. When I reached the errant craft, I hooked one arm over the side and headed back to shore. Lil had a fire roaring when I hit the campsite, which was fortunate, because I had absolutely no feeling from my navel down. Yes, it was a risky rescue. But the alternative was equally poor. I sure wouldn't recommend such action for people with coronary problems. Furthermore, anyone who lets his canoe drift off should be diagnosed as suffering from terminal stupidity.

North-country grouse furnish excellent fall sport and supply a superb source of fresh meat on a trip. In wilderness situations the canoe hunter can experience the nearest thing to virgin upland hunting. Many backcountry grouse flocks have seldom if ever had their population cycles disturbed by man. On many fall trips, we live mainly off the land, taking along only a few dried vegetables, fruits, and beverages.

Big game had been hunted by canoe for centuries before LaSalle poked the bow of his craft through the rice beds of Green Bay. Native hunters discovered it was as easy to spear moose from a waterborne stalk as from shore; deer driven off a point could be dispatched quickly from a canoe. Since big game will float in the water even when dead, it was no great problem to tow quarry to a handy rock ledge for butchering.

The rules of the hunt have become more refined, but the canoe is still popular for stalking moose. Easing through a morning mist with the dark brown outline of a thousand-pound bull emerging at point-blank range is enough to blow the cap off any hunter's adrenaline valve. On camera or look-see trips, we have paddled almost within touching distance of a big bull by an upwind approach, drifting when his head was up, sculling forward slowly when his head was down and he was feeding.

Moose hunting, any north-country guide will affirm, is only

sporting until the rifle goes off. From then on, it is sheer, backbreaking toil. Jeep Latourell, co-owner with Jim Pascoe of Wilderness Outfitters in Ely, has handled dozens of moose and is rated one of the most dexterous in skinning and packing. Jeep carries two knives and a regular meat saw, using a Buck Knife for boning and splitting, a very finely honed Randall blade for skinning. Procedure after eviscerating a moose is to skin out one side of the animal entirely, then quarter and bone the skinned-out half, using the hide to protect the meat from coming in contact with sand or dirt. The carcass is rolled over on the skin and the other side is skinned out, quartered, and boned. The meat is wrapped carefully in butcher's cheesecloth, rolled in a tarp, and hauled to the canoe by packboard. Each wrapped piece is hung separately at camp to chill and is subsequently packed out by canoe or float plane. A trophy head is skinned up the back to the base of the skull and the neck cut off, allowing plenty of hide in front to form an adequate cape to go with the mount. Somewhat easier on the packboard and in the canoe are just the palmated antlers.

We use canoes extensively in deer hunts where I live, not to shoot from, but to move hunters around and to pack deer out. A few years ago, eight of us packed into Knife Lake in four square-back canoes and set up a base camp. We organized our hunts by running all four canoes to one point, dropping off six hunters who would then slowly work their way to a pre-arranged spot a half-mile upwind where the other two hunters had towed the canoes. The reason the Knife Lake hunt stands out in my mind is that it typified one of the hazards of late fall trips: the possibility of getting caught in a freeze-up.

Two of our group went back out to civilization the first night with a nice buck. We hunted four days with the three other canoes before a blizzard tore down from the north, snow began piling up, and the temperature shot down to five above. We hastily broke camp and headed out, skidding four deer over the portages between trips with canoes and packs. About 1 P.M. we had made it down to the rapids below the Knife River, pausing for coffee and lunch while the driving flakes built white ridges on our parkas. Above the roar of the rapids, we heard the hum of a single motor, and out of the whirling white emerged a 17-foot square-back piloted by Dorothy Molter, the legendary sixtyish Lady of Knife Lake, freighting in the final load of winter supplies to her remote cabin.

"Hey, Dorothy," we yelled as she coasted up. "Can we give you a hand on the portage?"

"Don't need to portage," she said tersely, brushing snow from her bandana and jacket. With that, she yanked the four-buckle arctics off her sneakers, rolled up her blue jeans, grabbed the bowline of her Grumman, and waded up that rapids like it was midsummer. Great woman, that one.

Back in the 1930s, as an out-of-work vacationing nurse from Chicago, she canoed into the Knife Lake country, liked what she saw, and settled down to operate a little one-horse trading center and wilderness clinic, selling pop, candy, and ice to campers, and patching up sick or injured Indians and canoeists. Originally her dad, Cap Molter, helped her out. Since his death, she has lived some 40 years in the area alone.

In the 1960s, some fuzzy-headed desk jockey in the Forest Service decided Dorothy was a detriment to canoe country, sent in an appraiser, condemned her property at about 5¢ on the dollar, and told her she had to get out. The hue and cry that went up from guides, outfitters, and canoeists across the nation was heard in Washington by such stalwarts as Senator Hubert Humphrey (and some levelheaded upper-echelon Forest Service personnel) with the result that Dorothy was granted lifetime tenancy on her property. To those hundreds of canoeists who wrote letters and phoned Washington in her behalf, Dorothy has remained eternally grateful.

Dorothy, incidentally, formerly did some deer hunting during harsh winters, but not in the ordinary sense. When supplies ran short, she would listen for a timber-wolf pack to make a deer kill, snowshoe up to the scene, run the wolves off, and carve out whatever she needed at the time.

Chapter 13

Charting the Route

It was after supper and a bunch of the guides were sitting around Billy Zup's fishing camp talking about duck hunting when somebody brought up the time Stanley Owl went out in the middle of the night, located a couple of duck hunters lost up on the Bear Trap River, and brought them back.

"Hey, Stan," somebody asked. "How'd you ever find them guys in the dark without a compass?"

Stan looked thoughtful for a moment. "Indian doesn't need a compass," he said. "He always knows where he is."

The gang digested this. Then somebody asked, "You ever been lost, Stan?"

"Nope." His sunburnt face split open with a big grin. "Sometimes camp lost, sometimes canoe lost, but not Stan." He pointed down at his boots. "Stanley is right here."

And that is the literal truth. If you can reach down and pinch your leg, you are right there. But darn few of us have an infallible sense of direction, and few of us care to spend a day or a week in a canoe trying to figure out where we are. Which is why we carry a map, a compass, and in our heads the know-how to use both.

Quite often you see the statement that "using a map and

compass is simple." Well, if this were so, there wouldn't be so many books and pamphlets trying to tell how simple it is. Outside of Stanley, I can't think of a single guide I know who hasn't told about getting messed up on directions several times, even going astray by reading the map wrong. The tools and methods for charting and following a course are nearly foolproof. It's just that the Lord never saw fit to make a human being foolproof. But we can work at cutting our errors to a minimum.

Fortunately, all of the North American canoe country is mapped. You may find a few funny things on some of the maps, like a rapids that is more of a waterfall and a narrow spot in a river that is really a rapids, but mainly the maps are accurate. Topographic maps show watercourses, elevations, and some of the portages. But one problem is that maps come in different scales. The most common maps have four miles of terrain condensed to 1 inch of paper (1:250,000). But you'll also find maps drawn to larger scales: 1 mile to 1 inch (1:62,500); 1 mile to 1¼ inches (1:50,000) or 1 mile to 2½ inches (1:24,000). It is easier to read details on the larger scales, but they are also bulkier. On most trips we have one set of small-scale (1:250,000) maps for each canoe and one set of larger-scale maps for the group. Care must be taken to make the mental shift if you switch from a map of one scale to a map of another—say from four miles to the inch to one mile to the inch.

All maps carry legends with symbols, words, or both indicating important features of the terrain. They are listed on the map margin for reference. Rapids are marked with a line across a stream, the letter "R," and the word "Rapids" or lines running parallel in the stream. Falls may be a line with an "F," the word "Falls," or a line across with two points aiming downstream. A portage may be marked "P" or "Por." or just be shown as a dotted line. Lake elevations are usually printed on the main lakes and give you an idea of uphill-downhill between.

Brown contour lines show the land elevations. These vary with the scale. On a 1:62,500 map the lines will show an elevation interval of 20 feet. On a 1:250,000 map, it will be 100 feet. Since the map shows a view from overhead, and since the canoeist is on the water level, it takes a little practice to convert one point of view to the other. Along streams, contours can be a matter of life or death. The system used by most experienced canoeists is to make a profile of the stream well in advance of the trip, which will tell them if the route is navigable or not.

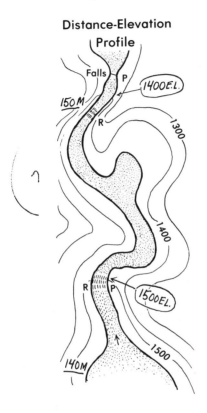

We use a magnifying glass to follow the course of the stream on the map, marking the elevation at each point where a contour line crosses. Then, using one of those little mileage wheels sold where maps or surveyor's supplies are available, we mark off every 10 miles of the river course with the accumulated mileage from the starting point. If we can't find our wheel, we mark 2½ inches on a section of fishline (2½ inches on the four-miles-to-the-inch scale is 10 miles, right?). We lay that hunk of line along the stream and mark each interval with a pen or pencil.

Now we have our distances for reference on the map and we also have the amount of drop for every 10 miles of river. If that drop runs from four to eight feet, it will probably be O.K., but if it gets to 10 feet or more per mile, it may be very treacherous. Where several contour lines crowd down to a narrow stretch, it indicates a canyon, and if there is considerable drop it could show a disaster area with no way to portage out of the canyon.

Some people hunt for such challenges, and they're welcome to them. If I detect considerable risk to my canoe, my outfit, or my epidermis, I ain't going, not with all the hundreds of other routes available.

In any downhill situation, care must be taken to locate a takeout point long before the canoe gets into treacherous water. Spring high water is particularly hairy. Few things are more terrifying than to get swept into a chute with no idea what lies below. A good many outfitters we know map their customers' trips upstream. This may mean a little more work, but the paddlers see every obstacle ahead clearly, and they can't go sailing over it.

Even following a slow, meandering river downstream can have its own problems. Where the rivers widen out into island-filled, grassy flats, or where they enter large, irregular lakes, the canoeist needs to know something about picking a route with the map alone and also picking a route with the map and compass.

Now let's say we are coming out of the Crowrock Bay of Otukamamoan Lake and heading for Trout River and the portage into Redgut Bay of Rainy Lake. We have a Mine Centre, Rainy River District, Ontario, map laid on top of a packsack facing the same direction we are traveling. There is just one gap in the wooded shoreline ahead, marked on the map with three little dots of islands (A). As we paddle past these we note the long bay to our right (B), and then, hanging to the right shore, we cross the W-shaped point and between the point and island (C). This looks something like that last bay we crossed, because we are looking right at the trees on the right shore, which seems to be a dead end. But the map shows a channel out of view behind that jutting point (D). So we push off and round the point. Sure enough, there's our channel, with some open water and islands beyond. In a half hour, we come out of the channel and pause by point (E), which is recognizable by a thin slot in its nose. From here we see nothing but a whole lot of irregular shoreline and what looks like bays, but our map tells us it is a bunch of islands, and beyond the biggest island lies the river. We figure our best bet is to keep along that right shore another mile to that rounded point (F), from where we

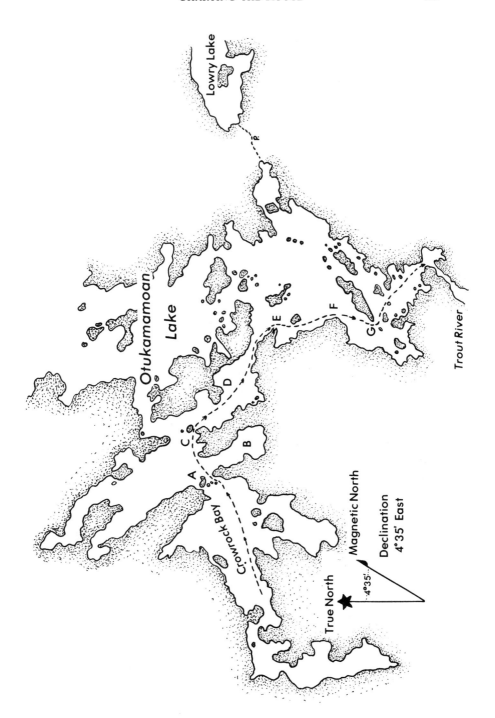

will be able to see the narrow tip (G) of the big island. So that's how we play it.

When we paddle around the tip, we see that small elongated island ahead, which looks like a projection of the shore. Our map shows that a line from where we are, across the end of that island and that little oval island beyond will hit the mouth of the river. So we simply sight across that little oval island, pick out a big pine landmark on the far shore, dig in our paddles, and head across the bay. At the halfway mark, the mouth of the river comes into view. With a laugh, we curve down into the channel to the portage.

Notice that we had no need for the compass. We went from a known point and carefully followed landmarks, arriving at our destination. That's how most canoe travel is done. But now let's go to a situation where we will be shooting a compass line.

We're coming down Manitoba's Gammon River into Aikens Lake. This is relatively flat country and there are a lot of weedy islands and bays. We want to cut right across the lake and hit the river; we don't want to waste time picking our way along the shore. Our campass is a plastic-base Silva with a movable dial. We lay the map flat and the compass on top of the map, ignoring that wavering magnetic needle for now. With the compass direction arrow pointing the way we want to go, we draw a line along the base plate from our known position (A) to the north tip of the big island (B), which lies directly in front of the river mouth. That tip of the island will be our reference point. When we reach there, the river mouth is just a half mile away.

With the base plate lying along our route line, we rotate the dial so the letter "N" is up and one of the meridian lines inside the dial coincides with a meridian line on the map. The top of a map is always north. The "N" on the compass is north. We have both aligned. Now we look where it says "Read Bearing Here" and we see the number 290. That is the true geographic bearing from where we are to the point of that distant island. but it isn't the compass bearing. The compass bearing is a magnetic bearing because the needle points to magnetic north. And this is why all this business isn't so simple: There are two norths. "True" or geographic north is the North Pole, the top end of the world, where all the meridian lines converge. But the magnetic lines on the earth converge at the magnetic pole, which moves around a little every year but is now on Bathhurst Island in the Arctic,

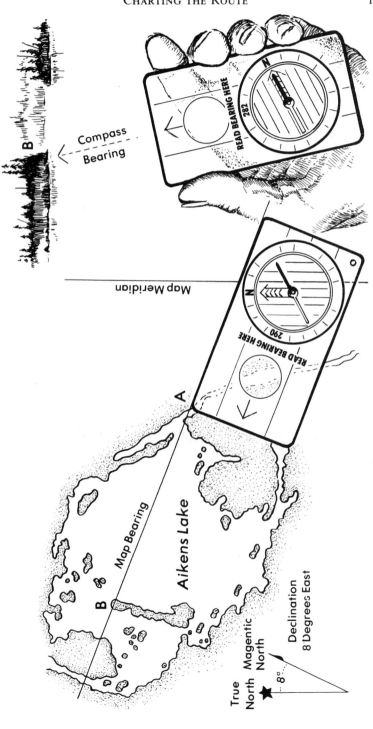

which is about 1,000 miles south of geographic north. And every compass in working order will coincide with a magnetic line leading to that pole. (Unless we do something silly like getting a knife or a fishing reel or something with iron in it too close and throw the magnetic needle off.) Maps are all printed in respect to true north, but the compass points to magnetic north. The difference between those readings is called the "declination" and is carried on the margin of most maps as a V-shaped symbol with the number of degrees east or west.

Now if we were heading straight north from the Grand Portage Indian Reservation, which is a little way from where I live, we wouldn't have to worry about that declination because magnetic north and true north would be almost in line. But when we move east or west, the situation quickly changes. For instance, a canoeist in northern Maine will find out that his map will have a declination of about 18 degrees west. That is, his compass needle will be pointing 18 degrees west of north. The farther north we go, the wilder it gets. In northern Alaska, the compass needle will be pointing northeast because that is where the north magnetic pole lies in relation to Alaska. If we somehow got to Ellef Ringnes Island (heaven forbid) we would discover that magnetic "north" on the compass was straight south!

But enough of that. Our map shows that our declination at Aikens Lake is about 8 degrees east. Which means that the compass needle is pointing 8 degrees farther to the right of the map than true north. So we have to subtract that 8 degrees in order to get our compass reading the same as the map and the terrain. Eight from 290 gives us 282 degrees, which is our magnetic bearing, and which is what we will be traveling. We rotate the dial to a bearing of 282 and with the compass flat in one hand, we turn it until the magnetic needle lines up with "N." Now we sight along the arrow that says "Read Bearing Here" and that arrow will be pointing across the water to the tip of the island. If we can see clearly enough, we pick out a clump of spruce on that bearing and paddle to it. If we can't see the other side very well (or at all, as in fog) we can lay the compass on the bottom of the canoe parallel to the keel line and paddle ahead, keeping the canoe aimed at bearing 282. We will come out pretty close to the tip of the island. From there we paddle across to the right-hand shore and follow it around the corner to the river. (Just a mile and a half ahead is a campsite and we still have time to get a mess of walleyes for supper.)

Sometimes we don't use a Silva compass. Sometimes we use a military "lensatic" compass that doesn't have a rotating dial. To make things easy, we carry a little plastic protractor in our map case. Let's see how it works with our Gammon Lake map. Where our bearing line intersects with a north-south meridian, we center the protractor. We see that the number of degrees between the two lines is 70. That is, our bearing is 70 degrees west of north, which on our compass is 290. O.K., we subtract that 8-degree east declination and have our magnetic bearing of 282. Holding the compass level, we bring it up to our eye, turning it slowly until 282 shows up clearly in the eyepiece of the lens. The top of the lens is slotted, like the back sight in a rifle. The cover has a thin wire fixed dead center. We line these two up and sight across the lake, getting a fix on that clump of spruce at the end of the island. We fold up the compass and map, paddle across the lake to our reference point, go around it, head over to the right-hand shore, and follow that into the Gammon River.

It is quite apparent that to follow any course, with or without a compass, we must keep an accurate record of where we started and what reference points we pass. We can do this with a pencil or in our heads. But we must keep track of our position on the terrain and on the map.

But let's suppose we didn't. Let's suppose that on our first lake, Otukamamoan, we went straight across the lake instead of south, paddled into the bay going toward Lowry Lake, thinking it was the mouth of the Trout River, and wound up at a dead end. Yikes! Of course, we can paddle right back out of that bay, but now all that water and those islands look alike. The first order of business is to get the lake and the map together. What we must do is get the map pointing north so we can make sense out of all the points and islands around us. North on the map is a bearing of 360 degrees. On Otukamamoan Lake, the variation is 4 degrees east. O.K., we lay our Silva compass on the map with the bearing arrow "N" and the dial meridian lines in line with one of the north-south map meridians. Then we turn the whole works until our magnetic needle points at 4 degrees. Oh, so now we are adding on 4 degrees. Yep. When we go from the map to a magnetic bearing and the variation is east, we subtract. So when we go from the magnetic bearing back to the map, we add.

Well, we have the map right with the lake, now where the heck are we? We can look back at that lousy dead-end bay. It runs east and west. Yeah, and right in the entrance is kind of a square-looking island. So now we hunt around the map. Aha! Behold and lo, there is our bay, island and all. And we start to laugh. For the love of Pete, instead of going south to the river, we paddled east, right across the lake. Well, sure. There to the south is that bunch of islands, and all we have to do now is pick our way through them into the mouth of the Trout River. But we won't pull any more klutzy tricks like losing track of where we are . . . no, sir.

Map and compass reading is simple? No it isn't. And we should be darn good at it before we get to heck and gone in the boonies. We must memorize the rule for declination when going from map to compass bearing: Subtract for east, add for west. And we must remember that the reverse is true when we go from a compass bearing back to the map. We don't have to be on the water to practice map work either. We can get a map of any local area, park, farmland, anywhere we can pick a known point and plot a course to another point, correct for the variation, and walk that compass bearing to see if we come out where we are supposed to.

Every state department of conservation and every Canadian provincial department of natural resources has maps of its lakes and streams. Topographic maps in the U.S. are available from the U.S. Geological Survey, 1200 S. Eads Street, Arlington, Va. 22202 for areas east of the Mississippi River and from the U.S. Geological Survey, Federal Center, Denver, Colo. 80225 for the West. U.S. Corps of Engineers offices in most major cities have detailed maps of rivers and lakes, but they do not show any but the most well-used portages in the remote areas. The Lake Survey Center, Department of Commerce, 630 Federal Building, Detroit, Mich. 48226, has hydrographic charts. Information on state waterway maps is available by writing the conservation department at the capital city of the state involved. Local canoe areas very often have some of the best-detailed maps, not only showing routes, but also campsites. In such areas as the Boundary Waters Canoe Area, where the Forest Service requires all camping to be done on designated sites, the Fisher Maps furnished by outfitters are an excellent aid, since all the sites are marked with red dots.

In Canada, the best source of maps is the Canada Map Office, 615 Booth Street, Ottawa, Ont. KIA OE9, where a list of all charts is available for every area of the nation in the 1:250,000 scale and some areas in the 1:50,000 scale. Write for current prices. Anyone wishing detailed aerial maps of a given area can mark the section to be covered on a topo map and mail it to the National Air Photo Library, 615 Booth Street, Ottawa, Ont. KIA OE9, after checking on prices. Add a note to your order indicating that the waterways are of chief interest, so that the clerk handling the order will select maps with a minimum of sun reflection appearing in the photos.

All of the Canadian provinces have maps of parks, recreation areas, and better-known canoe routes, available through the Departments of Lands and Forests, Tourism and Travel. The Canadian National Railways is an excellent source of information on trips that can be made by loading canoes and equipment at a point reached by road and then going by rail to a more remote area.

It is best to learn navigational skills in the better-known canoe areas prior to heading into the backcountry. In every situation, it pays to keep track of the route on the map, constantly checking and rechecking the terrain and direction as though our lives depend on it.

Which they do.

Chapter 14

Custom-Outfitted, Guided Trips

"The bass have moved out . . . we'll have to set up camp someplace else."

Little Rock, Arkansas, TV outdoor reporter Jerry McKinnis and tournament angler Bill Murray paddled inshore where guide Harry Lambirth was hustling up supper over a wood fire. Harry fed a couple of fresh sticks into the blaze and wiped his hand across his chin.

"The bass are here, all right. They just need a little urgin'."

Jerry and Bill had driven north to film some Ontario smallmouth-bass action and were on a very tight time schedule. With two canoe loads of cameras and sound equipment, they were understandably concerned over the success of the venture. Harry had packed the crew into the Darky River, which he considered one of the best September smallmouth spots. Although in his early twenties, Harry had logged more time in the bush with a canoe and spinning rod than most men experience in a lifetime. Briefly, Harry knew his business. And his business was guiding.

Two years prior to this trip, Harry had helped Jerry and Bill get a good film on Minnesota-Ontario border-lakes fishing. Experts with light tackle and maribou jigs, the Arkansas TV team had filmed thousands of feet of exciting bass action in shallow water.

On this, their return trip, they employed the same tackle and technique but without a hint of success. Reasonably enough, they assumed the bass were schooling in deeper water. Harry knew different. The bass had simply changed food preference.

Turning to with a stout stick, Harry poked through the shoreline marsh grass and, with a few well-placed smacks, laid out a half-dozen meadow frogs. One of these he rigged with a single hook through the nose, cast it near a half-submerged tree, and promptly belted an 18-inch slab-sided smallmouth bass. In short order the entire TV crew was tiptoeing along the shoreline like a line of herons, plucking unwary frogs from their weedy environment. Transferred to terminal tackle, the frogs were snapped up by greedy bass, the film action was shot, sound recorded, and the canoe safari concluded with smooth success.

The point here is not a comparison of fishing ability. Bill Murray and Jerry McKinnis are pros. Both have extensive experience as guides in the Arkansas-Missouri bass impoundments. Being pros, they recognize that the local guide, with intimate knowledge of his immediate area, can save even the most skillful angler a lot of time. In this instance, with a commercial venture at stake, the burden of success was on the guide. Harry was well paid for his work and got a fat tip besides. But it wasn't only the fishing that was involved. It was also the guide's job to get the canoe party in and out of the area without a hitch and to furnish a lightweight, comfortable camp and tasty meals. Harry ramrodded the whole show efficiently.

A good guide offers a service based on knowledge gained from experience. Similarly, the canoe outfitter (who may also be a guide) has watercraft, camping equipment, and a menu available based on what experience has taught him works best in his locality. Thus, a person outfitting for a river float in some southern river may find a local preference for a certain type of fiberglass canoe, which performs superbly on the sand, clay, and sunken-log waterway, while in the north he may be outfitted with aluminum craft to better withstand the grinding effects of the sharp granite underlying the streams and lakes of the Precambrian shield. Similarly, the paddle styles and camping methods of guides in one area may be radically different from those in another, although each may be an expert in his own environment. Guides and outfitters are often specialists. The sportsman who is seeking a trophy moose will require a completely different type of guide and outfit from the one required by a YMCA official leading a group of teenagers. The businessman taking his son on a wilderness fishing vacation has different requirements from a professional photographer seeking to film wildlife. Also, a professionally outfitted, guided trip is a crash course in wilderness living. It can be a valuable learning experience. The trouble is, it ain't cheap. But it isn't exorbitant, either.

An expert canoe guide will charge a fee ranging from $35 to $50 per day. Outfitting will range from $15 to $20 per day for each person, complete with watercraft, all camping equipment, and trail food. A family of four with a guide can expect to spend something in the neighborhood of $900 for a full week. Four men with a guide will be splitting the cost into fourths, which would run a little over $200 each. On top of this there will be licenses, and possibly camping fees and customs duty.

It doesn't take much mental arithmetic to figure out that a family could make a good down payment on canoes, tents, sleeping bags, and packsacks for what a completely outfitted, guided trip would cost. On the other hand, many people have neither the space nor the inclination to accumulate a lot of equipment. Or they may wish to sample several outfitters and make use of several guides before they make a purchase. Some people, with their own outfits, hire a guide only. Some, who have part of their outfit, such as tent and sleeping bags or canoe, may get a partial outfit from a commercial operator. Most competent outfitters will rent individual items, but the package rate for a complete outfit is usually 30 to 50 percent less than the rate for the separate items.

Assuming—as thousands of tourists do every year—that the services of a guide and outfitter will be used, how can you determine which outfitter and guide to select? On paper all outfitters are "The World's Greatest."

The poorest way is to drive to the area and make arrangements on the spot. This is done quite often, but most good outfitters have the bulk of their watercraft and equipment booked in advance. The best guides are booked well in advance, too. It is just good insurance to have the whole trip booked as far ahead as possible.

The nation's outdoor magazines carry advertisements from

dozens of competent North American outfitters. These people provide free folders listing their equipment, services, and rates. Some canoe manufacturers list liveries where their craft are available. Grumman publishes such a list. The sports and outdoor shows staged annually in cities across the U.S. and Canada feature displays by outfitters, most of whom man their own booths. Some potential canoe trippers will write to a few outfitters, compare rates and services in their folders, and then make a point of visiting these same operators at their sport-show booths to check out details.

If you want a particular emphasis on your trip, such as trout fishing, bear hunting, nature photography, or history, it pays to ask specific questions. The outfitter who has the knowledge will answer carefully. It is not reasonable, however, to expect an outfitter or guide to map out a detailed trip unless he has a deposit on the trip and the assurance that somebody is going to pay for his services. There are some people with all of their own equipment who will try to "pump" an outfitter or guide for free detailed trip information. This is tantamount to seeking free services from a doctor or asking an electrician to diagram the wiring for a new house. It is a quick way to turn them off. An outfitter has equipment and services to rent or sell. A guide has knowledge and skill. Neither will knowingly give it away.

So your first order of business is to establish your credibility with the outfitter and guide. After spelling out what you're looking for in the way of a vacation, you should then make clear your own experience and ability. The person who says, "I've had only very limited experience with a canoe and will need some good instruction," is quite easy to deal with. Any good guide or outfitter can teach basic canoe paddling in a few minutes. The person who is experienced in canoeing or camping or both has some very definite pluses that will affect the length and type of trip set up. However, now and again, somebody attempts to bluff his way with an outfitter, perhaps out of some mistaken feeling that he has to come on as a cross between Chief Pontiac and Paul Bunyan. This deception is pointless.

It is important to inform both outfitter and guide if anyone in the group has a disability that could affect travel or has an allergy to insects or some particular type of food. This is not uncommon, and the professional guide and outfitter will quickly adjust the trip, equipment, and food to meet the problem. Of course, anyone in the party requiring medication of any sort, such as a diabetic, should be sure to have his medical supplies packed.

Once I had a guide working for me who was allergic to, of all things, fish. He was young, tough, a good canoeman and camper, and he loved to catch fish. But if he ate as much as one mouthful his throat would swell up and he would be an immediate hospital case. His allergy even extended to touching fish with his bare hands, a contact that would make his hands turn red and swell up. He simply bore this affliction while filleting and cooking fish for his clients. He is currently a forester with a state conservation agency and still loves to catch fish, but very meticulously avoids eating any.

I have known several people who could be rendered unconscious by a bee sting. Such afflictions are fairly common but are difficult to believe. If someone has an acute insect allergy, most outfitters will recommend scheduling the trip during the very early spring or in the fall when the chances of contact are minimal. A strong reaction to poison ivy can cause the guide or outfitter to change a route or vacation time to avoid contact. In any event, it is best to lay all the cards on the table so that trip planning can include any contingencies. This includes the makeup of the groups in regard to age and sex. A trip with youngsters is planned differently from one with all adults.

What should the client expect from the outfitter? First, all equipment should be furnished as listed. If the references to equipment are in broad generalizations, it may be well to inquire about the make and weight of the canoes and the size and weight of the tents. It is perfectly legitimate to request separate tents for couples, if desired, or separate tents for parents and youngsters. Most outfitters include all equipment except rain gear, personal items, toilet articles, and towels. Outfitters who do furnish rain gear usually provide ponchos, which are not only unhandy when paddling but unhandy in the event the canoe swamps. It makes good sense for the client to bring his own rain suit or parka.

Most outfitters furnish a menu with choices of food for breakfast, lunch, and supper. If some people in the party have strong dislikes for certain foods, the menu should be carefully gone over and a consensus achieved before returning it to the outfitter. If there are no big food problems, it may be well to let the guide work out the menu, since he may have some specialties such as pies, cakes, fresh blueberry pancakes, or fish dinners.

In addition to a menu, the outfitter should furnish a checklist of staples and general items such as toilet paper, scrub pads, dish soap, salt and pepper, cooking oil, and matches. However, there is no point in packing unneeded items. If, for instance, the party prefers its coffee black, a notation should be made that cream and sugar for the coffee need not be included.

Sometimes an outfitter may be unable to get a certain food item during the season, although he has it listed on his menu. In this instance, it is common procedure for the outfitter to substitute what he has on hand. However, if there are a lot of substitutions on the menu, it may indicate that the outfitter is not quite the "World's Greatest" as advertised.

One advantage of hiring a guide is that the professionals in any area know their suppliers quite well. A guide will make sure that even a mediocre outfitter includes every necessary item. As a member of the state-certified staff that taught wilderness canoe guiding for many years in Minnesota, I admonished potential and working guides to run their own check on the equipment and food. If some necessary item is missing when the party is 40 miles into the bush, it is the guide, not the outfitter, who will bear the brunt of the party's wrath.

It should be made clear prior to the trip exactly what is included in the outfitting fee, and what, if anything, is an "extra." Customarily, extras include outboard motors, side-brackets, camp stoves, reflector ovens, and lanterns. Some outfitters charge extra for life jackets; some do not. You'll have no misunderstanding of costs involved if you request and pay the outfitting bill prior to the beginning of the trip. The guide is paid at the end of the trip.

The party has a responsibility to return all equipment in good condition. Any equipment damaged or lost by your party is your responsibility. You are expected to pay for repairs or replacement unless some type of breakage agreement or insurance is paid for in advance. Breakage includes damage to equipment caused by bears, storms, or just plain error. On the other hand, if the outfitter leaves out some significant item, the party is due a refund on that item.

There is a great difference in guides, and it has nothing to do with age, size, or ethnic origin. I have known well over a hundred commercial guides and have had more than a dozen handle clients for me when I was an outfitter. All of these guides had specialties. Some were excellent anglers, some had an uncanny knack at finding game. Some were superb outdoor chefs and could create a gourmet treat out of a few basic ingredients. Some were extraordinary packers, portaging loads that would buckle the knees of most mortals. Some were phenomenal paddlers. A few had a rare combination of specialties. But all of them had one thing in common: they liked people and sincerely strove to provide clients with a memorable wilderness trip.

Strictly from the business standpoint, every guide knows that a good trip means a happy client, probably a tip, and future trips from the same party or their friends. He also knows that a happy client makes the outfitter happy and results in more bookings. There are guides like old Bill Magie from Duluth who was still guiding in his 70s, not only on his experience and skill as a woodsman and canoeist, but also on his ability to tell an endless series of hilarious campfire stories without repeating himself. Ray Adams, an Ojibwa from Fort Frances, and one of the strongest packers I ever met, may not say three words all day. Most river guides in the Ozark country are colorful yarn-spinners. So are the Quebecois of the Laurentian north, even though they may talk all day in French knowing that the client cannot understand a word.

It is important to establish a good guide-client relationship. The best way to do this is to let the guide run the show. Let him know what type of trip you want, but don't tell him how to do his job.

The client who cheerfully pitches in on the camp chores is going to find a guide who will bust his britches to provide a good trip. The client who is a "good sport," who can take the vagaries of weather, the nuisance of insects, and the unpredictability of fish and game with good humor, will receive in return a maximum effort from his guide. The chronic complainer, the faultfinder, may get the bare minimum. Probably the worst move a client can make is to override a guide's judgment in such matters as seeking to cross a wind-ripped lake or insisting on riding down a piece of white water the guide feels is too dangerous.

As an outfitter, I had a standing agreement with every guide that I would back his judgment to the hilt. Any time a client began to countermand the guide, the trip was over, at the guide's discretion. I can recall only two occasions when this occurred, both times when young guides were leading parties of elderly men. In both instances, authority was quickly restored when the guide quietly informed the party that as far as he was concerned the trip was over, and he was packing up his outfit and heading back to the base. The choice of getting along with the guide or being left in the woods did not take long to decide. By the time the trips ended, the incidents were forgotten and each party was on excellent terms with the guide.

I can recall three times when parties came in and definitely lodged a complaint on a guide's behavior or performance. On one occasion, the guide was misunderstood; on one, the client was just flat wrong; on the third the guide was in error.

The occasion involving the misunderstanding was somewhat involved. The guide had a party of eight men, some of them elderly, in late fall when the water was cold. The men had chosen their own fishing partners but not on the basis of canoe ability. After two spills by clients, the guide arbitrarily paired the men off on the basis of canoe ability and told them to stay that way or else. The party thought the guide was doing something on the basis of fishing ability or was just being ornery. There were no further accidents, and nobody got into real trouble. Unfortunately, each of the men had some idea he was a heck of a canoeist, and the guide—who was quite young—had a tough time trying to convince some of them they weren't. They didn't understand what the guide had done until I explained his action after the trip. And I'm not sure that they even then accepted the explanation.

In the instance where the guide was dead right and the client wrong, I laid the facts of life before the client clearly and distinctly even at the risk of having the party go home sore. I underestimated the clients in that instance. After a quiet discussion, they admitted they were probably wrong, recognized the problem, and—to my surpirse—booked a trip for the following year.

The time the guide was wrong, I listened to the complaint and questioned the guide in private. Then I apologized to the party. Finally I sat down with the guide and asked him how he should have played it. By then he had already recognized that he'd blown the trip and had also figured out how he could have avoided the problem.

Most guides discover over the years that people who book trips into a wilderness area are generally a pretty reasonable segment of citizenry. In the first place, people who book a canoe trip recognize that there are certain inherent factors of hardship involved, and they are willing to take that risk. They do not expect flush toilets and maid service in the bush. Also, people who seek wilderness adventure are basically more interested in establishing a friendship with the outdoor world, not attempting to "conquer" it. In this respect, both guide and client are starting out with an identical outlook.

Chapter 15

Tricks of Fate

Among the many inhabitants of the Ojibwa spirit world, two are very much in business today: Naniboujou the trickster, and Wendigo the killer. Every treacherous set of rapids or dangerous waterfall has a Wendigo ready to snatch the unwary paddler to total destruction. Naniboujou, on the other hand, is the spook who tips the hot tea pail on your hand when you are stoking the fire or slips the fillet knife out of its sheath so you slice the ball of your thumb when you reach in the packsack for the utensil kit. Mostly he engages in deceit, like taking a rain jacket out of its pouch and leaving it back on the last portage; but he has a lot of evil kinfolk who will jab your stomach to cause cramps or slip sand inside a boot to raise a blister.

Caucasian students of Indian lore assert that the Ojibwa invented these spirits for psychological catharsis—to transfer blame and avoid self-incrimination and guilt. Which goes to show how dumb some white men are who have never traveled the canoe trails. All of us who paddle and portage are on daily speaking terms with Naniboujou, and many of us have encoun-

tered a Wendigo. Once I looked one right in the eye and got away
. . . but that's a tale for later on. There is no 100 percent foolproof
insurance you can get to ward off these marauders. But an alert
canoeist can raise his own odds, and he can pack nostrums and
patching materials along to repair damages to the physique.

Among the educational opportunities open to canoeists, none
are more valuable than comprehensive courses in first aid offered
by the Red Cross and various state departments of health and
education. These courses are usually taught at night through the
local schools and at minimal expense. Some hardy paddlers are
certain in their own minds that no mishap will ever befall them on
the trail, and they may be right. But there is no certainty that some
careless driver won't ram their car on the highway going to or
coming from a trip. So a working knowledge of first aid might not
only reduce pain and damage but could also save a life.
Furthermore, there is always the possibility of coming upon some
other canoe party in deep trouble, where first aid can be of
considerable value.

Just down the lake a piece from our cabin is the Charles L.
Sommers Wilderness Canoe Base, operated by the Boy Scouts of
America. It is the radio-directed center for the most comprehensive search-and-rescue operation in the Superior-Quetico area. On
24-hour standby is a fully trained, fully equipped "Ready Team"
set to go at a moment's notice, summer or winter. Coordinated
with Minnesota's Lake and St. Louis county sheriff's departments,
local game wardens, Northern Lakes Aviation, and the Ely
hospital staff, it operates by canoe, boat, and float plane in the
summer, and by ski, snowshoe, snowmobile, and ski-plane in
the winter. In an average year, the Ready Team will handle 50 to
80 injured, sick, or lost wilderness travelers.

Those of us who serve as volunteers with this group are
fortunate enough to meet and hear some of the best-trained U.S.
and Canadian military experts on wilderness survival, who
occasionally lecture at the base. Every attempt is made to keep up
to date on constantly changing first-aid procedure. Anyone who
was in the armed forces, say 30 years ago, will quickly recognize
that some accepted battlefield procedures of that era are now
considered not only obsolete, but possibly damaging to a victim.
The use of a tourniquet to stop bleeding, now recognized as highly
hazardous, is a case in point. Alcohol-based medication such as

iodine or Merthiolate was dutifully daubed on open wounds until research indicated it destroyed more tissue than it saved. As knowledge increases and medication improves, more changes will take place in first-aid procedure; thus anyone who has taken a course should go back periodically and absorb new methods as they develop.

Most first aid on the trail involves the treatment of relatively simple complaints: headaches, constipation, diarrhea, insect bites, cuts, sprains, minor burns, blisters, and wayward fishhooks. But there is always the chance of a drowning, broken limbs, heart attack, dislocations, or severe burns and the accompanying deadly shock that can follow. I will not attempt here to give a ten-minute course in first aid. It cannot be done. However, in addition to your taking a good training course, consider a few publications that might be of value, including the popular "Red Cross First Aid Text Book," Kodet and Angier's "Being Your Own Wilderness Doctor," and the comprehensive "Emergency Treatment and Management" by doctors Thomas Flint, Jr. and Harvey M. Cain.

In all first-aid courses, emphasis is always laid on the "first" aspect of treatment, and that only a doctor is competent to administer to an involved problem. In search-and-rescue work, we are taught to (1) assess the situation, (2) make a plan, and (3) act on the plan. This is good procedure on any problem, large or small. It concentrates thinking, saves time, coordinates effort, and reassures the victim. Where a serious problem occurs, a decision must be quickly made whether the victim can be moved to where help is available or whether help must be brought in. Injuries to the spine, for instance, can be aggravated to instant death if the victim is improperly moved.

So now another factor becomes readily apparent: on any wilderness trip, it behooves the planners to determine in advance (from governmental agencies, ranger stations, outfitters, other canoeists, and good maps) what villages, ranger stations, fishing camps, roads, railroads, mines, or logging operations may be on or near the route, and to mark these on the map. Government and private flying services have fire-patrol and supply routes that crisscross much of the northern canoe country, and these should be noted. Practically everyone who lives or works in the wilderness is versed in emergency procedure and will know what to do once contact has been made. Therefore the canoeist should know where to seek assistance in regard to his map position and what procedure to follow.

In every instance where outside help is needed, the person or persons seeking help should have a slip of paper on which is clearly written the name, age, and sex of victim; home address; location (as accurately as possible); type of known or suspected injury; and any treatment given. Nothing is more frustrating to a search-and rescue team than to have some wild-eyed, tattered canoeman come staggering out of the bush to announce: "We gotta have help . . . Al is up in the woods with a busted leg . . . hurt real bad. . . ." And then he can't tell you what lake Al is on. In the instance where somebody paddles out for help and meets a motorboat, the note can be passed along. But do not assume if one person or party is told, that help is on the way. Give identical messages to every person contacted until you're assured that the message has gotten through. Search-and-rescue teams do not mind getting a half-dozen calls concerning the same mishap. But it is disconcerting to get a single message that is a few days old.

Specific distress signals are used in the wilderness to attract attention from passing aircraft or boats and to pinpoint the location of the victim for rescue parties. Again, it is well to have as many of these distress signals as possible in view.

Three of anything in the wilderness is a trouble call: three T-shirts hung on three poles spaced out along the shore; three canoes tied in a triangle, keels up in the water or on the shore with an orange tarp stretched over them can be seen a great distance; three persons waving paddles in unison, particularly if they have something white or orange tied to the paddle; and three fires spaced along the shore with plenty of green leaves and twigs thrown on to create three columns of thick smoke. Other signals are distress flares, orange dye markers, and the shiny metal mirror in the toilet kit. With a little practice, mirror flash can be directed a considerable distance, but it should cease once the plane has started down for a look. No pilot likes to come in with a bright flash blinding him on approach.

In all cases where a rescue operation is involved, whether a bush pilot or government plane, boat, or overland operation, the rescued people must understand that *all costs are their responsibility. There simply are no free rescues—emergency or otherwise.*

It is not reasonable to expect the taxpayer or any private

individual to foot the cost for some canoe party's mistake. The influx of inexperienced canoeists into the far north and accompanying problems, as well as an uncooperative attitude by some toward paying the costs of bailing them out of their jams, has resulted in an increasingly critical outlook by Canadian authorities toward allowing these trips to continue. If the klutzy canoeist does not soon shape up, it is quite possible that future trips in or near the Arctic may be stopped, or else a sizable bond may be required before a group is allowed to go.

Back to first aid: every canoeist with a lick of brains has a good first-aid kit. Unfortunately, most commercial pocket kits available over the counter have a lot of stuff you may not need and often leave out some very necessary items. In search-and-rescue work, we have developed a kit for canoe trips that covers most of the smaller problems and contains items easily obtainable from the corner drugstore. Here is our list: 2 dozen Band-Aids, 1 dozen large and 1 dozen small butterfly closures, roll of 2-inch gauze bandage, roll of 1-inch gauze bandage, 6 gauze pads 4 × 4, 6 eye pads, 12 various-sized Telfa Pads, roll of 1-inch Dermicel tape, 3-inch Ace elastic bandage, 2-inch and 3-inch Coban bandages, four tongue depressors, 1 pair tweezers, 1 scalpel, 1 single-edge razor blade with cardboard sheath, germicidal soap, ointment such as Mycitracin, 6 large safety pins, aspirin, laxative, a dozen kitchen matches waterproofed, and a small note pad and pencil (for those emergency messages, hey?). All this is packed inside a heavy-gauge plastic bag, which is rolled up tight and sealed with two big rubber bands. The list may be expanded depending on the makeup of the party, length of trip, and remoteness of the area. The kit goes in a pocket on the frame pack or side of gear pack.

In addition, we have other items that serve double duty. The long-nosed pliers with sidecutters for taking hooks out of fish also remove misdirected hooks from human hide. Each canoeist carries a 30-inch bandana, excellent for slings or for tying up sprains. Each person has a sharp pocketknife and a length of eighth-inch nylon line, the line valuable for lashing splints and immobilizing ankle sprains outside the boot.

Also, all persons who have any kind of an allergy or affliction must have their medication on them and protected. Some diabetic canoeists we know carry their medication inside plastic Kodak film containers taped shut and strung around their necks. All canoeists should have a current tetanus immunization. There is an old wives' tale that tetanus or "lockjaw" is caused by getting cut on something rusty. That may or may not be true. Tetanus is a little bacillus that lives in the ground and in animal feces, and it can be encountered anywhere that dirt gets into a wound. Dr. Julius Kowalski of Princeton, Illinois, an enthusiastic canoeman and author of many articles on medicine in the outdoors, is a real bear on tetanus immunization. He has carried his little black bag to many conventions of outdoor writers and has administered shots to every scribe who could not recall being immunized. Immunization is usually effective for several years after treatment. Your family doctor or clinic should have a record of this and can tell if your immunization is current.

Another malady, every bit as deadly and much more common, is called hypothermia, the modern term for what used to be called "exposure." Hypothermia occurs when heat is transferred from the body and body temperature drops below the normal 98.6 degrees. It can happen even in summer when a canoe swamps and the occupants are immersed for more than a few minutes in cold water, and it can happen when soaked canoeists come out of the water into cool, windy weather. It can also happen when canoeists get wet from rain or snow while paddling in cool weather. There is a widely held belief that hypothermia is induced by freezing weather. This is only partly true. Hypothermia is most often a threat during wet, cool, windy situations.

When the body temperature drops just a few degrees, a change takes place within the body to conserve heat around the vital heart and lungs. Circulation to the extremities, including the head, is reduced. You have absolutely no control over this change. First symptoms include slurred speech, apathy, prolonged shivering, and a lack of coordination. Continued deterioration results in hallucinations, convulsions, and death.

Once the body is chilled, it cannot regain normal temperature unless an outside heat source is provided. A hot sun can help, but a fire is quicker. This is one reason every member of the canoe party should be carrying a waterproof container of matches. In an emergency, the patient can be stripped down, dried, and placed in a sleeping bag with a warm, dry person whose body heat will be absorbed. If the patient is conscious, hot drinks such as tea, coffee, or just hot water can help. The canoeist who travels in the spring or fall when the water is icy, or at any time when a wet, windy, cool situation exists, must recognize that hypothermia is as close as the tip of his paddle.

And now, as I promised earlier, I will tell you about my encounter with a Wendigo. I will not tell you where this one lives, because just as sure as water flows downhill, somebody will rush right out for a challenge. Suffice it to say, he lives in a rapids, one of a series of five below a waterfall. He dozes much of the late summer and fall, but he is quite alert and active in the spring when the water is high and booming northward toward Hudson Bay.

In this instance, Lil and I were completing a canoe film. We had adequate footage of paddling, camping, fishing, and cooking, but the director felt a little white-water action would spice up the show. The camera was set up on a ledge below the falls, and the director (who was also the star) prepared to push off solo in his 15-foot canoe and ride down the rapids in a shower of foam and glory. It was at this point that a Huron guide, our good friend Stanley Owl, appeared packing over the trail and paused to ask, "What are you doing?"

I explained to Stan that we were filming my ride down the rapids.

"Can't make that one." Stan poked a brown finger at the chute. "Tried that once . . . got busted up."

At that time, as a man in my thirties, I was at my peak of confidence. Perhaps over the peak. With a condescending smile I said, "You just watch me, Stan." And I pushed off while Lil, on shore, held down the button on the 16mm. Bolex.

The first drop was in two stages, a five-foot crack in a ledge, a hard right and another crack into a few standing waves, a second chute with haystacks, and then three more less turbulent drops. I ferried to position, lined up the chute, and let 'er go. To this day I believe I could have made it if a gust of wind hadn't sluiced the bow sideways (or maybe the Wendigo grabbed it). In any event, canoe and I missed the center of the chute, shot over the ledge, and plunged nose-first into the fuzz. I jammed my head forward under the thwart and hung on as we hit. The canoe was an old-style aluminum model with air compartments fore and aft. As we smacked bottom, part of the bow was torn out and all forward flotation vanished—which I was not aware of at the time. The underside of that rapids was like a huge automatic washer, a whirling maelstrom of suds. I felt the Wendigo grab at my legs, ripping my pants, and one of his fingers tore my wool shirt from the pocket to my belt. His fist smacked both my knee caps trailing outside the canoe, and it sounded like his teeth were chewing the whole forward part of the hull into tinfoil.

The canoe, of course, with only stern flotation remaining, was slow in coming up, but it finally did. I got one breath of air before we went over the next drop and the Wendigo jerked the canoe and me to the bottom again. We were further banged and buffeted until the stern wallowed up to open air and I coughed up half the river. With the third chute coming up, I decided to abandon ship, which I did with alacrity. In a dozen strokes I was not only out of the water but into the woods. It is amazing what a human can do when thoroughly scared.

When we finally retrieved the canoe, it had six holes, several broken ribs, and a cracked keel with no more structural strength than a soggy noodle. Stanley helped me pound out the hull and tape it up so Lil and I could make it back to civilization. To his credit, he never said a word, although I did detect a hint of a smile as he looked over the damaged craft and my tattered clothes.

The Wendigo? Yep, he missed that one time. But he is still there. Waiting.

Chapter 16

Mukwah and Associates

As all canoeists discover, there are some things in the outdoors that will "getcha."

The first danger anticipated by the neophyte is an attack from a bear. Fortunately, Mukwah is not aggressively antisocial. A different situation exists on those watercourses in the far north where an unpredictable polar bear or grizzly may be encountered. However, all the real or imaginary wildlife hazards lumped together make only an insignificant fraction of the real danger on a canoe trip, which is driving up and driving home on the highway. Compared to pavement, the wilderness is the safest place on earth. There are, however, a few nuisances that should be considered.

In many parks and forests, prominently displayed signs carry the message "Do Not Feed the Wildlife." This is sage advice. Unfortunately, it is often impossible to avoid feeding them; that is, the minute species such as the mosquito and the blackfly, which inhabit almost all of the northern canoe routes. Of these two predators, the blackfly or gnat is considered the meanest. First, the blackfly is a sneak: he issues no warning hum. He stalks silently, lands imperceptibly, and swiftly gnaws through the epidermis, the derma, and into the blood cells below. He will not attack openly, but often creeps in a cowardly fashion under the hat brim, or up the shirtsleeve or pants, cuff, and upon completion of his vampirical assault will stealthily depart, leaving a blood smear, a welt, and an agonizing itch. Furthermore, blackflies often travel by squadron, and when the leader peels off for the kill, the entire formation swoops down.

In addition to causing itching and running sores, blackflies secrete a venom that can cause listlessness, nausea, and even serious illness. People with insect allergies may swell up, with legs looking like blotched balloons or faces like basketballs. Those of us who live in blackfly country usually develop an immunity, after soaking up quarts of venom, but the newcomer should be prepared. Some repellents that seem to work include BF-100, made by LJB Laboratories, 1001 E. Cass Street, St. John, Mich. 48879; G.I. repellent, made for the U.S. military forces, which is sometimes available in surplus stores; Cutters; and Sportsmate. The best repellent, however, is clothing. Canoeists who prefer brief shorts and no shirts are welcome on any trip we take because they will draw off the bulk of the flies. For ourselves, we use heavy pants pegged into wool sox, leather boots, thick wool or flannel shirts with the sleeve gaps sewn shut, and a hat. People particularly susceptible wear bandanas around their necks, cotton gloves, and sometimes head nets.

Much the same apparel works with mosquitos, and nearly all commercial repellents are successful. When the potion reads, "Repels Mosquitos," they stay away, which leads one to believe they are functionally literate. Without a good repellent, you soon learn that mosquitos are no fun. We can only marvel at the hardiness of the ancient fur traders who had only the wind in the daytime and an eye-smarting smudge at night to keep them off.

A mosquito in the tent at night is another matter. It is not the bite that causes irritation, but the whine of his motor, usually revving up about the time you're dozing off. One procedure is to call an air-raid alert, going into action with a flashlight in one hand and aerosol bomb in the other. While effective, the lethal spray is not recommended for the sinuses in close quarters, and the solvents in the spray, at point-blank range, may have a devastating effect on the tent fabric. A better method is to give the tent a couple of shots of spray an hour or so prior to turning in. By bedtime the tiny biters will be listed in the obituaries and the poison will be dispersed in the air.

Another thing: printed on each spray can is the legend, "Caution: Flammable. Do Not Use Near Fire or Flame." The manufacturer ain't kidding. Each year a number of tents are charred and campers partially barbecued by bug bombs fired off too close to a lighted candle or lantern.

Other winged pests are local, seasonal, or both. They include the common housefly, which hangs around campsites and occasionally hitches canoe rides while dining on the paddler's legs and ankles. Repellents work only so-so on these pests. Sand fleas, or deerflies, are larger hot-weather critters usually found adjacent to waterways. While repellents are effective against them, they have a nasty habit of working up under the hairline to gnaw on the scalp, and they'll bite right through ordinary cotton sox or shirts. For sheer bravery, they are unsupassed in the insect world. They will keep on biting even when slapped and only cease their attack when completely mashed.

Chiggers in the South and Midwest, and noseeums in the North, invade in battalion strength. Chiggers infest the undergrowth and are often picked up if you stretch out on a grassy spot. Noseeums will go right through a tent screen. The before-bedtime spray will handle noseeums. Repellent around the pants cuffs and belt line will usually discourage chiggers.

Spiders are seldom a problem, but they do occur and they can bite. Spider bites are painful and can cause nausea, particularly among youngsters. Spiders don't hunt for people. People get bitten when they disturb the spider.

Bees, hornets, and wasps are very mean, but can usually be seen and avoided. Round, paperlike nests hanging from branches, infested tree hollows, and grayish deposits of mud on the underside of old buildings are all areas to stay away from. The best defense is sometimes a pair of fast feet, although we have fought wasps to a standstill with the bug bomb. Bites are painful. Bee stingers are left in the wound and should be removed by scraping rather than plucking. Cold mud on a sting will "slow" the hurt. Multiple stings may require medical help.

Leeches are often encountered when dragging a canoe up a muddy stream or over a beaver dam. If they have become well attached, a cigarette, match, salt, ammonia, or alcohol will help loosen their grip. Infection is the main danger from a leech bite. The wound should be cleaned and covered with a Band-Aid.

Canoeists in the Southwest must be on the lookout for centipedes and scorpions. The stings are similar to those of bees or wasps, but more painful and debilitating. Cold packs slow the spread of venom, but medical attention is often required. These critters like to crawl into or under things. It pays to shake out boots, pants and jackets before putting them on, and to shake out sleeping bags and mats daily. Tents with floors and zip-up screen doors will keep them out.

Ticks often ambush canoeists. The most common type is the wood tick, which starts out like a small bran flake on your skin and swells up like a marble. The swelling, of course, is your blood, acquired when the tick burrows his head under your skin. Ticks can be removed by applying alcohol or ammonia or by burning. At tick time, a small bottle of alcohol or ammonia can be included in the first-aid kit. Where ticks are abundant, it pays to strip down and check your body before turning in at night. Repellents will help keep ticks off.

Ants, such as the fire ant in the South, can cause problems with campers, particularly kids. Usually, they are quite visible and can be avoided. Kids sometimes get bitten when they take a stick to "stir up" an ants' nest. An inspection of a campsite will reveal any infestation. In the South, it is best to get local information on the current situation.

So much for bugs. They are usually the chief wildlife problem on a canoe trip, but there are a few others, including our old friend, Mukwah. Though the black bear is rarely a problem with people, he is quite often a problem with tents and packsacks. The claws on a bear's front pads are like steel hooks, and they can open a heavy Duluth bag with one swipe or slash the side of a tent like a razor. A bear will do this only if the food pack is left on the ground and the tent is zipped shut. Bears usually arrive on a food raid when the campers are gone for a while. We rope our food packs up by tossing a line over a handy limb or by running a line between two trees, the pack suspended in the middle. To get the pack up high enough, one of us pulls on the rope while the other boosts the pack with a stout stick. We use the stick to get the pack higher than our reach because a good-sized bear has the same reach.

Tents are left open, the flaps tied back so any visiting bear can enter, look around, and leave without making a new door or removing the front screen. If a nuisance bear is hanging around, some guides try to eliminate the problem with a bug bomb. Dick Rietman and Andy Hill, who used to guide for me, carried an extra, half-used aerosol bomb as bear insurance. In camp, they tied a strip of bacon around the can with fish line and set the bait in a prominent spot. Any bear that wandered into camp would first try to get the bacon loose; failing this, he would bite right through bacon, bomb and all. The ensuing explosion of escaping gas not only cleared Mukwah's sinuses but usually cleared him out of the area bodily.

Johnny Nikkenen, who guided in our part of the country for a couple of decades, swears by ammonia. He says he has placed a small bottle of ammonia up under the flap of the food pack, cracked the cap open slightly so the fumes would drift out, and never had a bear go near the pack. This sounds reasonable, but I have not personally tested it out.

Firecrackers will frighten bears away but in some places are illegal. They also are a fire hazard in dry woods. Most bears will run just by being yelled at. I have seen Lil take an armload of rocks and attack a marauding bear with a few choice threats that sent the bandit racing into the forest in sheer terror. But then, we know a little about bears. Each one is an individual. Some spook easily, some don't. Mama bears with cubs are usually touchy. You never know if they will run away or come in swinging—or pretend they are swinging. Bears are great bluffers. But bluff or otherwise, we avoid bears with cubs.

Occasionally, Mukwah will exhibit strange behavior. In 1968 we outfitted a young couple for a honeymoon canoe trip up to Ashigan Lake. One morning, while breakfast was on the fire, a bear made a run through their camp, scooped up a Duluth pack like a football, and ran into the woods. Whether the couple or the bear was more surprised is open to debate. The pack contained no food, only extra clothing. When they regained their composure, the couple cautiously followed the path taken by the bear; sox, handkerchiefs, shirts, and women's underthings were strewn along the route, the empty Duluth pack at the end where the bear threw it in disgust.

My neighbor Harry was camped on an island once and witnessed a bruiser of a bear invade a camp on a point of land directly opposite. The campers were out fishing and had taken the precaution of roping the food pack high. The frustrated bear marched back and forth under the pack, finally let out a bellow of anger, and proceeded to stamp the tent flat. He didn't just knock it down, he stamped on it. This is the only time we have known a black bear to do anything like that.

About 1970, an Army lieutenant and his wife came up for a week's canoe trip. The route they selected passed through an area where we knew a black raider was operating. We marked the general trouble spot on the officer's map and told him to either pass through there without camping or else rope his food high. The couple were back in four days, food gone, and a packsack lacerated. The visibly embarrassed officer avoided the subject, but his wife gleefully related the adventure. On the second night, the wife pointed out that they were in the area where the bear was indicated on the map and that maybe they should rope up the food pack. The lieutenant said he had a better idea. He lashed the pack to the center thwart on the canoe and turned the canoe upside down. "If a bear tries to steal the pack, the noise will wake me up and I will chase him away," he promised.

At about midnight, they were awakened by a goshawful clatter. Peering out of the tent, they saw a huge bear dragging off the food pack, canoe and all. At dawn, the campers crept out and found the canoe about 200 yards away, the pack torn to shreds and all their food gone. Luckily, the canoe had suffered nothing but a few dents, and the lieutenant and his wife managed to return to base in a day and a half, subsisting on lake water and a pocketful of raisins.

Some guides rate the moose as the only dangerous critter in the woods. Bulls can be ornery during the fall rutting season, and an occasional cow will get belligerently protective of a new calf in the spring. Moose are not particularly bright, and their vision is somewhat less than 20-20. In myopic anger, they may challenge an intruder. A loud shout will sometimes halt their advance. But if this tactic fails, the only retreat is to the canoe or up a tree. Fortunately, moose are not numerous, and even seeing one (unless on a hunt) is a rarity. The bold one is extremely rare.

Small creatures of the forest—squirrels, chipmunks, and mice— probably inflict more damage to food and equipment than do the big animals. Every campsite has some sort of four-footed wildlife in residence, and most of them will invade a packsack to nibble holes in plastic packets, holes through the Rye Krisp, and holes through the roll of toilet paper. These Lilliputian pack bandits can be thwarted by keeping the packs tied, zipped tight, and slung high. They will seldom eat through the thick canvas on a Duluth pack, but we have had them chew through good nylon bags on pack frames and even through a tent corner.

Mice do weird things on tents at night. At a few well-infested campsites, we have had the little buggers get their kicks by climbing to the peak, then sliding in sheer delight down the slick nylon fabric . . . all night long. Or until somebody shook the tent with authority, which usually ended the frolic.

Bigger rodents, such as porcupines, are fond of gnawing on paddles, particularly where perspiration from the hands has left a salt deposit. These relatively peaceful creatures with their pack of darts seldom pose a threat to humans, but they can be a real threat to any dog along on a trip. I twice have assisted in the removal of quills from dogs, and it was no fun for any of us. It took two people to hold each dog down and one to pull out the quills with a pair of pliers.

Snakes are a concern in some southern and western areas, but fortunately there are no poisonous species over most of the north. In 1949, wildlife biologist George Arthur and I were floating Missouri's Current River in pursuit of smallmouth bass. It was my turn on the stern paddle while George was casting the pools ahead. As we moved around a huge blown-down oak, I grabbed a limb to hold the canoe steady. As I drowsily watched George retrieve his spinner, a movement next to me brought my senses alert. About 18 inches from my left hand, a thick, dusty mocassin was flattened along the limb. We eyed each other briefly as I quickly released my grip and the canoe floated away. While I have seen dozens of water snakes on canoe trips, this was the only time

I ever encountered a poisonous one. Fortunately, canoe routes in most snake areas are on streams where roads, farms, and gas stations are often nearby. Anyone who does get bitten can usually get to medical help. Residents who canoe snake country regularly are likely to carry antivenom kits.

Snake bites, however, are extremely rare, and snake fatalities are considerably less numerous than those caused by bee stings.

Hour for hour, the camper who travels the canoe trails is measurably safer than he is while driving the family car.

Chapter 17

Family and Group Canoe Trips

Like a regiment of weary, grey-green ghosts, the shoreline fir trees dripped in the cold, early-May drizzle. Wisps of mist rose from the slick black lake surface as our canoe hull eased up against the granite ledge below the campsite. Jess climbed over the side of the canoe onto the shore, beads of water glistening on the yellow nylon rain jacket zipped up to her neck. She grinned as I hefted the four gold-and-black walleyes on the stringer. "You want to help me clean these for dinner?" I asked.

Jess nodded, backhanding a trickle of rainwater running from her nose. It was the opening weekend of the 1975 fishing season. We were camped on Adventure Lake, between Ely and the Gunflint Trail. My granddaughter Jess was on her first canoe trip. She was two years old.

One month later, my mother and I were portaging into Ensign Lake for a day's bass action. I carried the canoe and the lunch pack, Mom toted life jackets, fish rods, and landing net. She insisted on "packing her share." My mother is in her 80s.

There is nothing particularly remarkable about either of these incidents, but they indicate one of the more obvious changes that has overtaken the canoe scene during the last two decades: the wilderness is no longer the private domain of a few hairy packers in patched canvas pants. Well, maybe it never was. Long before my European ancestors arrived in New England, my wife's Indian kinfolk traveled and camped on America's rivers in family units. Outside a few areas of the far north where this same tradition continues, today's family camping is mainly recreational. Fun is what it's all about.

One benefit of being an outfitter was the opportunity to meet hundreds of family units both before and after their trips. Most families came back tanned, shiny-eyed, and overflowing with the wonder of the outdoors. Some came back with the attitude that they had endured an interesting adventure that they would rather not repeat. For a few families, the trips were disasters. For the families whose trips became disasters, there was probably nothing Lil and I could have done to avert discord. Wilderness camping is simply not everybody's cup of tea. It is pretty hard to "make" people into canoe campers if they are dead set against it. If part of the family is in open rebellion against the activity, the chances are no one will have much fun.

Wind, rain, and insects can whammy a trip. If these are not enough reasons, the disgruntled camper can invent several dozen more to turn the vacation into a complete bummer. But so much for the negative aspects. It might be profitable to analyze the elements that seem to create the climate for a good family trip:

Family Council. In most successful ventures, all members of the family had a part in planning, going over folders and maps, comparing one area against another. Somebody kept score with a pencil, listing the chief points of interest, until choices were narrowed down and a vote was taken.

Special Interests Considered. Not all members of a family are gung-ho fishermen or marathon paddlers. Room is made in the planning for activities such as swimming, rock hunting, animal and bird study. Sources are searched for a history of the area and historic sites are noted on the map.

Shakedown Cruise. Prior to heading into the wilderness, many families take a few canoe rides down nearby rivers or test their camping skills in state parks or county campgrounds. If some members of the family have previous experience through Boy Scout and Girl Scout trips, YMCA, churches, and other organizations, this is a plus.

Reading Up. There are few up-to-date canoe-camping books around, but there are some excellent magazines, including *Canoe, Backpacker, Boys' Life,* and *Camping Journal,* and some occasional articles in *Outdoor Life, Field & Stream, Sports Afield,* and *Popular Science.* A scrapbook of articles makes a handy reference.

Leadership. There has to be one ramrod, no matter how democratic the organization, and this is usually Poppa, although there can be a dual authority. Somebody has to have a final say-so and veto power if discipline is needed.

Assigned Jobs. Camp chores can be split up according to age and ability, with the little guys gathering wood, hauling water, and drying dishes. Everybody pulls his weight as much as possible. Equipment makers have recently come out with kids' packs like Camp Trails' "Me Too" and the Kelty Sleeping Bag Carrier. Gerry has a padded pack frame Kiddie Pack in which to deposit the tiny tots so they can be carried over a portage. Older kids can take turns at turning out a full meal over a fire, pitching their own tent, and charting the course with map and compass.

Setting Reasonable Goals. Where youngsters are involved, canoe speed records are ignored. Travel is punctuated with frequent stops to poke along the shoreline, feed the chipmunks, inspect beaver dams, observe ducks with broods, and occasionally to pause on a sand beach for a midday swim. In an ordinary day's travel with small kids, 6 to 10 miles is a good average, depending on the number of portages and whether the trip is by stream or across lakes. With youngsters in the teen range, 10 to 25 miles may be possible.

Selecting a Campsite. With small children on a trip, there is no substitute for an island. They can't wander off the island and get lost. If the shoreline is at all steep, the kids are zipped up tight in their PFDs. A check is made of the campsite for overhanging deadfalls and other hazards. Last fall, granddaughter Jess and I were in Ontario, lake-trout fishing from the shore, where we had

pulled the canoe up against a steep granite bluff. I was busy
getting the lunch together when the little squirt vanished. As I
looked up and down the shore to see where she went, a tiny voice
called down from the bluff overhead, "I'm guck!" Which was her
version of "I'm stuck!" She had climbed up 20 feet, from
handhold to handhold, until she could get neither up nor down.
Grandpa had to retrieve her.

Sharp knives and axes are kept sheathed and out of reach.
When fishing is over for the day, hooks are snipped off the lines
and stowed in the tackle box, which is stuffed into a pack. While it
might seem that there are a multitude of dangers to kids on a
canoe safari, there are far fewer than they meet around the
average city yard. At least I have never heard of a kid getting hit
by a car in the wilderness.

PLANNING GROUP TRIPS

There are hundreds of thousands of canoe campers on the
continent's waterways today who were first introduced to the
outdoors through trips sponsored by the Boy Scouts, Girl Scouts,
YMCA, YWCA, Boy's Clubs, churches, schools, and summer
camps. We can never adequately thank that ever-changing army
of dedicated leaders, both paid and volunteer, who have helped
instill an appreciation of our outdoor heritage in generation after
generation of young adventurers. Those of us who make our living
as guides and outfitters have been fortunate to associate with
outstanding leaders from those groups, and to observe some
highly successful group canoe operations. A sampling of these
may provide some insight for organizations and leaders who may
be starting youth-group canoe ventures.

One of the most successful has been the High Adventure
Program of the Boy Scouts of America. National in scope, the five
units include: Maine National High Adventure Area, Box 150,
Orrington, Maine 04474; Northern Wisconsin National Canoe
Base, Boulder Junction, Wisconsin (mailing address: 720 Franklin
Square, Suite 200-A, Michigan City, Indiana 46360); Florida
Gateway to High Adventure, 2960 Coral Way, Miami, Florida
33145; and the Charles Sommers Wilderness Canoe Base, Box
509, Ely, Minn. 55731. These facilities offer a wide range of

canoe experience from freshwater trout and bass fishing to alligator study in the Everglades. Since I am most familiar with the Sommers operation near my home, a brief examination of that program may be of some value.

Leadership gets top priority. Each group of nine canoeists includes one adult advisor plus one trained guide or naturalist from the base. The group travels in three 17-foot canoes, three persons and their equipment to each craft. Camping units are contained in two 8 x 10 tents holding four and five persons respectively. Crews are balanced with both strong and inexperienced paddlers in each canoe. Every crew has a turn at directing the route with compass and map. Camp chores such as fire building, cooking, and sanitation are rotated. Safety gets high priority, with each canoeist required to meet swimming qualifications and each required to wear a PFD while traveling. Each member must submit a standard Scout medical report, a requisite for personal sickness and accident insurance policies.

Each guide is also a member of the Scout Base Ready Team, a radio-directed, 50-member arm of the Lake County, Minnesota, search-and-rescue program. Few emergencies involve base-sponsored trips, but the Ready Team regularly hits the trail to assist other canoeists with problems.

The Chicago Boys Clubs, specifically the Valentine Boys Club and the McCormick Boys Club, regularly conduct wilderness canoe trips under a program started in 1972 by Gene Bahde, assisted by Marc Dosogne and Steve Murray. Trips are set up for 12 days. This allows one-day return, leaving ten days on the trail. Stiff requirements include a medical checkup one week prior to departure, ability to swim ¼ mile, some prior camping experience, attendance at all club camping, canoeing, and first-aid training sessions, participation in all fund-raising activities, and a sincere interest in canoe camping in a group atmosphere. To offset trip costs, club members hold car washes, bake sales, candy sales, and dances, with the help of staff members and parents. Canoe trips are arranged in ten-person units, with eight boys and two staff members. Close communications are maintained with the outfitter. Reservations and food lists are set six months in advance with a follow-up confirmation just prior to the trip. All necessary papers are in order for tax exemptions. Free Minnesota fishing licenses granted to youth-group members under 16 years of age are obtained in advance. Parents are provided with a list of personal items for each youngster, including toilet articles and clothing. Strongest points with the Boys Club program are trained leadership and detailed organization.

Bernie Halver, the experienced canoe camp Scoutmaster for Troop 257, Overland Park, Kansas, an outstanding example of an unpaid volunteer leader, has spent many years of his spare time instilling high standards of personal conduct in the outdoors.

Troop 257 has 11 parents including 7 drivers and private cars to move the 30 or more trip members from home to the canoe area. Each driver is fully insured, and each acts as an adult advisor on the canoe trails. Through various contacts, the troop arranges to bunk in overnight on the road at a military base on the way north and at a private home on the return, breaking up the 750-mile drive into two days. In addition, meals are scheduled ahead at churches in those areas. Women's groups serve a filling supper for $1.50 each and a solid breakfast the next morning at $1.25.

On the canoe routes, the group is broken into units of 10 or fewer canoeists, including adult leaders. In addition to standard Boy Scout Health and Medical Records, each youngster has written consent for the trip from parents and is given a complete list of costs (paid in advance) plus all activities that will be available, merit-badge pursuits, and strict rules of conduct and safety. Dress while canoeing is optional, but on the road all Scouts are in full uniform.

A different type of unit, which conducted canoe trips for many years in the north, is the Chicago Navy League, headed by Lt. Commander Donald Martinson. The league, composed of cadet sons of present or former members of the U.S. Navy, learns seamanship on the Great Lakes. While a canoe is a far cry from a torpedo boat, the summer camping cruises were a means of building comradeship, and at the same time learning outdoor skills.

In Oklahoma City, Oklahoma, there is an organization known as the "Camping 84th," which is the designation of Boy Scout Troop 84. Organized by Tom Yarbro 12 years ago, the troop is now operating under Scoutmaster Larry Foree, Assistant Scoutmaster Bob Stipes, and Adult Patrol Leader Dwight Weir. While the chief emphasis has been on backpacking trips ranging from

Canada to New Mexico, in 1976 the group took an Ontario canoe trip organized by canoe chairman John McBride. A total of 42 Scouts and adults made the nine-day trip for $62.50 per person, including the 2400-mile round-trip bus ride, meals, and canoe rental. Each member has his own camping outfit, and the group buys and packs its own trail food.

The bus is backed by three support pickup trucks in contact by CB radio. The group drove straight through to the canoe area, stopping only for meals and rotating drivers. Two of the pickup trucks pull U-Haul trailers with the camping gear. To save meal time, one pickup moves out ahead of the convoy, selecting a restaurant and negotiating with the owner to serve 42 suppers. Picnic lunches are set up in roadside parks.

A doctor, druggist, or drug salesman has been included on each trip committee, insuring that the first-aid kit is properly stocked. The trip has a medical officer who is trained in first-aid, but because of good organization and discipline he is seldom needed. On the 1976 canoe trip, the greatest injury incurred by any of the 42 members was covered with a Band-Aid.

And there, briefly, are some successful group canoe programs. Though these have dealt with boys' groups, the same holds true for the nation's growing numbers of women canoeists. The ideal was never better phrased than in the words of the founders of Troop 84, that "with motivation, discipline, and training, there is no limit to what a young person can do."

Chapter 18

Trail Clothing

Justine Kerfoot, the much-respected guide and proprietress of Gunflint Outfitters at Grand Marais, once told us how she booked a trip from a large organization whose members arrived on schedule, picked up their maps and equipment, loaded their canoes on the beach, and then proceeded to remove every stitch of clothing before paddling down the lake. Justine said she had no bias either for or against nudist clubs, but she thought that it would have been a little less startling had there been advance notice. She cited this incident as an example of what might be considered ultralight outfitting in the clothing department.

Few people who live in the woods see much wrong with the human figure the way the Lord created it. If an individual wants to chance sunburn and extend a luncheon invitation to every bug in the woods, that's his business. We have also seen people in mid-July with goose-down parkas and four-buckle overshoes crammed into packsacks, which might be construed as the other extreme. Most canoeists who have no clothing hangups simply travel with light, comfortable garb, reasonably insured against weather emergencies. There is nothing difficult about this. Clothing is fitted to the region and the season, with some modifications for personal preference.

It is standard procedure to describe wearing apparel from the skin out, starting with underwear. Most guides, however, think from the outside in, which is the way the wind and weather strike. The periphery garment, then, should be light, windproof, waterproof, and of the best quality you can afford. Rain gear is the most important item of apparel the canoeist owns. Prices can be steep, especially for suits made of Gore-Tex,® but excellent outfits made of urethane-coated nylon are available for quite a bit less. The cheaper suits should be examined to make sure they have ventilation openings under the arms.

Within recent years there have been a variety of new fabrics created that are breathable, allowing condensation to escape but preventing rain from coming in. Some top suits are made by Peter Storm of Norwalk, Connecticut; Macbean of Scotland (handled by Recreational Equipment, Inc.); Grundens of Sweden; and the Gore-Tex outfits put out by Trail Tech of New York. Beware of those jacket and "chaps" outfits made up for backpackers. They are fine if you paddle standing up, but sitting down you wind up with a soaked lap and tail end.

For simplicity and good protection, many canoeists favor three-quarter-length jackets. Prices begin fairly low, with tougher, better protection as the cost climbs. One advantage of the parka is that cold rainwater, which collects in the lap, simply collects; there is no pants zipper opening for it to leak through with sudden and breathtaking results. When you shop for a parka, it pays to try it on in a sitting position to see if the skirt is long enough to cover your knees. Also see that there is room inside the hood to accommodate a hat. Good rain outfits, suits, or parkas, have wrist closures; these are a necessity when paddling in the rain because the water will otherwise run down inside the sleeves every time you raise the paddle for the start of a new stroke.

Ponchos are the cheapest type of rain cover and the unhandiest in a canoe. They billow out in the wind and are a real hazard in the water if the canoe swamps. But they are better than no rain gear at all—and they do make a nice camp tarp to keep the kindling dry.

Plastic rain suits are low-priced, available at any dime store, roll up into tiny, lightweight packets, and are excellent as long as it never rains. Anyone forced to wear one will find that they rip on every snag along the portage and do a superb job of condensing body perspiration, sometimes creating a much wetter situation inside the parka than out. They are the only rain outfits worse than a poncho.

Occasionally you run across handy young folk who wear only waist-length rain jackets, letting their lower extremities take a wetting. And if this is their bag, fine. Like all paddle pushers, we have had our share of cold and wet, but we don't seek it out. If we can stay warm and dry, we will go that route every time—and wet pants ain't part of our plan.

The windproof, rainproof exterior may be considered the outside layer of a protective clothing system that conserves or releases heat as the body requires. That layer, and the layers beneath, down to the skin, can be removed or added one by one to achieve a desired temperature, depending on the weather and amount of exertion.

Until the advent of synthetic fibers, the two best clothing insulators were wool and down. A lightweight down jacket is very warm, but it has no insulating property when wet. In summer, we use a knit wool sweater over a tight-weave wool shirt for cool days, adding the rain jacket if the nights are cold. Sweaters can be crammed into a corner or pocket of a pack on hot days.

Shirts and pants offer a lot of leeway in selection. We tend to favor Pendleton and Woolrich wool shirts, not only because they are light and warm, but because bugs don't bite through them as they do through thin cotton shirts. There are some excellent combinations of wool and synthetic fibers that wear better than pure wool. Pants made of tough whipcord or denim are good. We prefer green synthetic-fiber work pants, heavy enough to break a mosquito's beak.

In summer weather, we use cotton underwear, sometimes adding net long johns or quilted insulated outfits if we are 'way north. Frosty nights, it is nice to have the quilted underwear jacket for hanging half out of the sleeping bag while reading by candlelight. For cold, windy days on the water, the long-john pants help keep the legs warm. In canoeing, unlike backpacking, the legs do little exertion, and while the upper torso may be warm with scant cover, the legs can develop gargantuan goose bumps.

Our preference in sox runs to wool combined with synthetic

fibers, from 12 to 14 inches in length. The addition of nylon or acrylic makes the sox wear better inside the boots, and the warmth is still there, even when wet. Thick sox keep insects off the ankles and long sox can be pulled up over the pants cuffs to seal the legs off completely from the vampires.

On an ordinary two-week trip, we take only one set of clothing, one extra pair of sox each. We wash out sox every other day. On a sunshiny wash day, we don our swim suits, scrub all the clothes in a bucket at the campsite, hang them, dry them, and put them back on. It beats hauling extra clothes around.

There are many preferences in shoes and boots. River runners, who may spend more time awash than afloat, understandably prefer something like sneakers, which allow maximum agility in the canoe or in the drink. But sneakers or mocassins are not much good on rocky north-country portages. There is simply not enough ankle protection. For summer we like leather, mocassin-toe boots, 8 inches high and noninsulated. There is little advantage in buying the most expensive pair around. Boots are going to get wet constantly and should be kept treated with a good leather oil. The oil won't keep the water out, since it usually comes in over the top, but the oil allows the boot to dry soft and pliable and it helps preserve the leather and stitching.

Vibram or rubber soles, cleated for traction on mud or rocks, are preferred by many paddlers. Welt construction, with the sole double-stitched from the outside, like the Goodyear or Norwegian styles, are not only durable but also allow resoling. Once I purchased a very expensive pair of fine kangaroo-skin boots and was very disappointed to discover, when the bottoms gave out, that they could not be resoled.

So much for summer wear in the north. Spring and fall (or Arctic travel) may call for a different set-up. The same windproof, rainproof exterior is required, the underlayers are increased, or a good insulated parka is included. Those cotton or polyester pants, which are comfortable in the summer, now require plenty of under-insulation and can even be replaced by wool pants. Insulated boots, either with or without liners, keep the feet warm even when wet. Wool sox up to 22 or 23 inches in height offer more leg warmth. Foot warmth is more critical in aluminum canoes, since the metal is an excellent conductor of cold from the water.

In early fall, we stick with the layered, insulated leather boot. When ice along the shoreline doesn't melt during the day, we go to rubber-bottom pacs with an insulated liner that can be pulled out and dried at night. Felt liners work, but they tend to soak up perspiration. Inner "booties" made of Polargard, sandwiched between two layers of Dacron, will collect moisture on the outside next to the boot but will stay dry and warm next to your foot. We sew our own, but a few manufacturers are starting to make them— such as Recreational Equipment, Inc., and Columbia Sportswear, Seattle, Wash.

In very cold, wet situations, a good PolarGaurd jacket is valuable. Again, goose down offers fine insulation, but it must be kept dry or the protection vanishes. In early spring or late fall, when wind-driven snow howls around the canoe, the Polargard parka or vest is a handy item. And either will stuff pretty well into a pack when not in use.

Along about here, somebody is going to say: "Yeah, that klutz hasn't said anything about hands and head. Does he go bare-headed and barehanded when it's freezing?"

No, I don't. I don't go bareheaded in the summer, either. One reason is that my once-abundant cranial cover, which I combed and groomed so diligently during my college days, has now thinned to a fringe arrangement. Without cover, the top of my head gets sunburnt and bug-bitten in the summer and frostbitten in the winter, so I have a good collection of hats. Most of the time I prefer a soft felt hat with a wide brim to keep the rain and sun out of my eyes. Billed caps work fine, and some guides prefer knit caps or tams. When wearing headgear without a bill or brim, it is nearly always necessary to wear sunglasses.

In the hand-cover category, some canoeists wear a pair of cotton gloves in warm weather until their hands toughen up. Since I chop my home supply of firewood every year, I don't have that problem. However, cold weather is another bag of apples. Since there is no easy way to keep water away from the hands while paddling, we use wool gloves because they don't draw heat from the body like wet cotton. The trouble is, wet wool gloves tend to wear out quickly. Some beaver trappers use a rubber glove over wool liners, some go to leather mittens with wool liners. We go with wool and synthetic-fiber gloves when ice starts to build up on the paddle shafts. The synthetics do not slip around on the shaft like rubber and they dry out quickly.

One more item in passing: Sitting in a canoe in cold weather will compress even the best-insulated underwear, which means cold is conducted through the seat of the pants, resulting in a chilly bottom. Some cold-weather paddlers effectively use a square of closed-cell foam lashed in for a canoe seat liner. Regularly neglecting one's bottom in cold weather is not only uncomfortable; it can also guarantee a trip to Hemorrhoid Heaven.

Chapter 19

Repairs on the Trail

The late-afternoon sun was just beginning to nudge its way into the wedge of birch and balsam that flank Jasper Creek to the east of our cabin, when the metallic thump of canoe hulls indicated that a man I'll call Eddie, his wife, and two sons had paddled in from their trip. In a few moments, they trudged up the hill from the dock into the outfitting lodge and dropped their Duluth packs on the shaded porch.

"How'd it go?" I asked.

"Had a good trip," Eddie replied. "Well, up to today. We had a little problem coming in today and cut a hole in one canoe."

There is no word that freezes the arteries of an outfitter more quickly than the word "hole."

"Not in that new fifteen-footer?" I asked with growing apprehension.

"Yeah, I'm afraid it was," Eddie admitted. "But we got it fixed up and paddled in O.K."

About that time one of our guides, Mike Banovertz, came up

from the dock area where he had been repairing outboards. "Better take a look at the new canoe," he whispered to me. "It's got more than a cut."

The 15-footer was tied alongside the dock. That is, the bow half was tied alongside the dock. The stern half went off toward the middle of the lake at an angle of about 10 degrees. The canoe had been broken at the center, the left gunwale sheared, the hull cut to the keel on the left side, the keel bent, the right gunwale bent, and the right section of hull accordion-pleated. Obviously somebody had gone between two boulders sideways, had broken the hull, then pulled it up on shore and pried it and hammered it with rocks to get it back in some semblance of shape. Luckily, they had a roll of plumber's duct tape along, which was used to seal up the worst part of the rip. The fact that they paddled that crooked hull in was something to marvel at. But I didn't marvel very long.

Of course, Eddie paid for the canoe. That is, he paid $250 for the replacement. Outfitters will take ordinary dents and cuts in stride, but a structural break puts the canoe out of the rental business. Eddie became the owner of a 15-foot wreck, which we strapped to the roof of his car for the 600-mile ride south to Chicago.

While he was more than a little perturbed about having to replace the canoe, his wife kept giggling in the background. "You're taking this pretty well," I said to her when Eddie was out of earshot.

"It's really funny," she said. "We had already portaged around that rapids but Eddie decided he wanted the boys to go back up and run it with the empty canoe so he could get it on our home-movie film. The boys were tired and didn't want to do it, but Eddie insisted. They dumped in the rapids, the canoe broke, and we wind up with a wreck and a $250 film sequence."

Later I got a letter from Eddie that a good aluminum man had straightened and welded the hull and it was being used by the boys on a northern-Illinois river. There is no particular moral in this story. The point is, they had the foresight to take along a roll of duct tape for an emergency. When that emergency occurred, the tape got them out of the woods. Not in style, maybe, but out.

Every canoeist who has his head on straight will be sure to include repair materials whenever he is going on any kind of a wilderness trip. A repair kit often means the difference between paddling out and walking out. As old-time angler Art McCracken told me one time, "Yer seat'll outwear yer feet any day, sonny."

Every camping-trip repair kit should include items that can be used to mend canoes, paddles, packs, tents, clothing, and sleeping gear. Obviously, if a person decided to take along everything needed to do a factory job he would need an extra canoe just to haul spare parts and tools. We take a compact, lightweight outfit that will handle the problems for the canoe and equipment on that particular trip and will fit into a pocket or pouch. A few carefully selected items, plus a little ingenuity and "make do," go a long way.

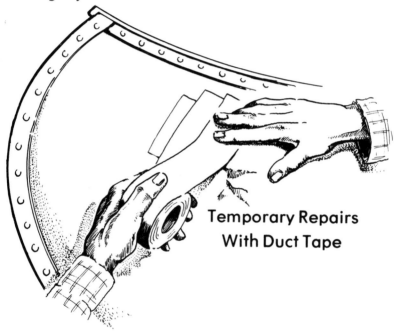

Temporary Repairs
With Duct Tape

To start with, let's take the most frequently damaged item—the canoe. Pretty fair temporary repairs can be managed on just about any hull with a roll of plumber's duct tape, the 2-inch stuff. It will stick to almost any surface and is extremely tough and fairly impervious to water. For cracks, cuts, splits, small holes, gouges, and nicks it is the ticket. However, it does not have much structural strength and cannot do a good job by itself in plugging up big holes.

Aluminum canoes are fairly easy to mend, even severely damaged ones. It is seldom that a section of hull is completely knocked out. The metal will tear and bend, but usually it will all hang together and can be banged back into reasonable shape with two smooth rocks, one held against the hull inside at the point of damage, and the other used outside like a hammer, similar to the method body-and-fender experts use to beat out dents in cars. Once the tear is pounded back into shape, the crack can be taped over.

Liquid metal that comes in tubes can also help patch small leaks. To improve sticking, the wound is sandpapered back an inch or so to remove the grime or corrosion. There are problems with liquid aluminum. It will not seal a large injury to the hull, it takes some preparation to ensure its sticking and it's not easy to remove later when permanent repairs are made to the hull.

On some aluminum canoes, such as Grumman, bulkheads are fastened in with small bolts and nuts. These have a tendency to loosen, particularly from vibration of an outboard motor. If so, a leak will result. It takes a Phillips screwdriver to tighten the bolts, so a smaller screwdriver with both regular and Phillips heads is handy. Those same bulkhead bolts are where the most consistent points of contact are made with bottom rocks. The recurring smack may not tear a hole, but it grinds off the aluminum next to the bolt to cause a crack and a leak. Cracks like these and similar small leaks along the keel are difficult to spot with the naked eye. If the canoe is propped rightside up on a couple of logs and filled with a few buckets of water, leaks can usually be detected. Tape doesn't work too well on bulkhead bolts in rocky streams, because the rocks keep knocking the tape loose or tearing it off. Liquid metal works well on these.

Thwart bolts and screws in the yoke pads can work loose. It pays to inspect these points from time to time. If a yoke pad comes loose, two canoeists can repair it, one squeezing the pad flat, the other wrapping it with duct tape. If it is not pushed flat before taping, the tape will start coming loose when the pad is compressed while portaging.

A pocket repair kit for an aluminum canoe should contain a screwdriver (Phillips and regular heads), pliers, extra bulkhead and thwart bolts, a roll of duct tape, a small tube of liquid metal, and a piece of sandpaper.

Wood-and-canvas canoes can be more easily cut or punctured than metal or plastic, but they are not difficult to fix. A kit for repairs could include that handy roll of duct tape, a tube or bottle of Ambroid (glue used in building model airplanes), a tube of waterproof Elmer's glue, some canvas, sandpaper, copper or brass tacks, a square of thin copper sheet, and a small coil of copper wire. Small cuts can be filled with Ambroid, spread on and worked into the canvas. Larger cuts can be sealed temporarily with duct tape. Later, at camp, the duct tape can be removed. A piece of canvas is cut to extend an inch beyond the injury on all sides and slipped into the hole between the skin and the planking. Center the patch and liberally cover the edges with Ambroid. Then press the torn canvas into place. A row of tacks along each side of the rip will secure it. We have also had good success by gluing the underpatch, sanding the surface, and gluing on a top patch, using no tacks. The edges of the top patch can be sanded smooth and painted over later.

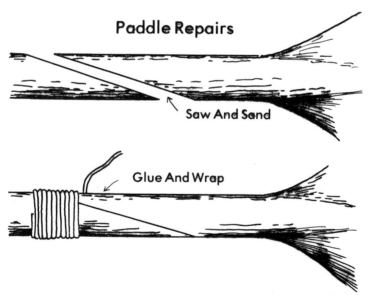

Paddle Repairs

Saw And Sand

Glue And Wrap

Broken planking can be reset by applying Elmer's glue to the splintered edges and pushing the wood back into place. We have found that a hole in the planking can be reset and glued, and a strip of copper sheeting cut to fit between the ribs, glued and tacked into place to add strength to the damaged area.

While discussing wood, broken paddles could be considered. There is the spare, of course, but if somebody breaks that one, you've got a real problem. Some books tell you how to hack a paddle out of a tree with an axe, and a lot of us have done it. But the process is very time-consuming, and the result seldom compares to a good Clement. To repair a broken paddle handle, saw or whittle the sides diagonally back from the break and smooth them out so the handle is straight. Sand them smooth and glue in place with epoxy, or Elmer's, using fish line to hold everything in place while it sets. When dry, wrap it with fish line or fine wire, keeping a layer of glue a half-inch ahead of the wrap. The diagonal cut will shorten the paddle about four inches, but it is better than no paddle at all.

If the canoe is fiberglass, the paddlers should have fiberglass patching and can also do a first-rate repair job on the paddle handle with that. A fiberglass repair kit includes sandpaper, polyester resin and catalyst, mat, and acetone cloth.

Soaked With Catalized Resin When Applied

Cardboard
Backup   Cellophane Sheet   Hole Trimmed And Sanded   Fiberglass Cloth
Taped Inside   Fiberglass Mat Layers   Outside Layer
                                    Overlap To Fill Hole

Patching A Fiberglass Canoe

To repair a fiberglass canoe, clean up the break on the inside and sand-paper back 2 inches or more around the edge. Layers of fiberglass mat, well wetted out with resin, build up the break, the first layer just covering the hole and each successive layer overlapping the last. When the patch is built up slightly higher than the surface, a piece of dry cloth is quickly laid over the last wet mat and ironed out firmly with a squeegee, the spatula from the cook kit, or something flat. Prior to the trip, practice fiberglassing should be done at home to get familiar with procedure. An excellent source book is "How To Repair Fiber Glass Boats" at $3 a copy from the Ferro Corporation, Fiber Glass Division, Fiber Glass Road, Nashville, Tenn. 37211. Small repair kits are usually available from fiberglass canoe dealers. And duct tape is a must.

The new ABS plastics, such as Oltonar, have special repair materials available from dealers. Kevlar canoes, which have a fiberglass sandwich, can be repaired by sanding off the Kevlar to reach the glass. In most instances, it is best to use enough duct tape to get out of the woods and then consult a dealer.

After canoes and paddles, tents are next in line for Purple Hearts. Tent injuries include punctures, cuts, abrasions, pulled seams, and torn-out peg loops and guy tabs. Tape will make good temporary repairs on cuts, with two layers of tape (one inside and outside) for a rainproof seal. Better yet are two pieces of rip-stop nylon patching, lapping about an inch on all sides of the injury and glued in place with fabric cement. Pulled seams or torn peg loops and tabs must be sewn back. Tabs often tear out with a piece of tent fabric, which means a section of nylon patching must be folded over and sewn in to support the tab. Webbing, thin nylon rope, or even a stout shoelace can be used for a tab loop.

Zippers on the tent screen can cause trouble. One common complaint is a zipper that "gaps" open after it has been zipped shut. This may be caused by dirt or by a worn zipper slide. To clean a zipper, unzip it all the way and brush the zipper teeth carefully on both sides with a toothbrush. If this doesn't do the job, take the pliers and pinch down firmly on each side of the zipper slide, squeezing it together just a smidge. If the gap still occurs, try squeezing down a little more. This will usually suffice to the end of the trip, until the zipper can be replaced. If the zipper fails altogether, sew the tapes together with temporary stitches, leaving a crawl-through space that can be secured with a few safety pins at night.

In our sewing kit we have four needles (two large for heavy tent work, two small for light fabric and clothing), a thimble, two spools of thread (one size 50 nylon for light work and a size 20 for heavy duty), a half-dozen assorted buttons for shirts, a dozen large-to-medium safety pins, and a small tube of fabric cement, all rolled up in a square foot or so of rip-stop nylon. To make the kit more compact, we wind the thread off the wood spools onto flat pieces of cardboard. The kit is stowed in a plastic pouch and fastened with rubber bands.

For emergency repairs to canoes when there is no tape or repair kit, the old voyageur's stickum is still available—pitch. This is sap from a balsam or spruce obtained by scraping away the bark at one spot so the tree will "bleed." The sap is gathered with a knife, placed in a metal container, and heated with a small amount of cooking grease to make it easier to handle. We have plugged holes by using alternate layers of pitch and shirttail patching. However, that is a very messy way to be fixing a canoe when tape is so cheap and easy to carry. Furthermore, it means injury to the live trees and leaves scars.

Chapter 20

The Last Campfire

Friend, we have covered a fair piece of the trail together in the course of this book. Since this is the last camp Lil and I will pitch before the end of the trip, let's mug-up with a fresh pot of coffee, lean our tired backs against a couple of accommodating pines, and trade a few thoughts on what this canoeing is all about. The previous 19 chapters have covered the technical aspects—equipment and how to use it. But all that does not explain the irresistible urge that draws us back to the water each spring as we watch winter's ice turn black and shatter in the breakup. It's something intangible but every bit as real.

Somehow over the years, as the bow of our craft curved mile-on-mile through bulrush-lined channels, split the shimmering reflections of towering lakeside bluffs, and slammed across cresting wind-driven waves, Lil and I have absorbed a feeling of kinship for our canoe and developed a suspicion that perhaps the Anishinabe are not far wrong in their belief that a spirit indeed dwells therein. Certainly, those times when we drove our paddles hard in unison to cross a wide expanse of lake or plunged headlong into the frothy throat of a thundering chute, our canoe was impatiently urging us forward. We have also come to realize that our craft is a subtle teacher, patiently unraveling the mysteries of seamanship at a pace we could absorb and constantly testing to determine how well we are learning. Perhaps it has been the closeness of the water, combined with the responsiveness of the craft, that has drawn us closer and closer together until we become almost a single unit of muscle, paddle, and hull.

These observations contain a few fragments of the picture, but there is much more. One June day we were crossing the last long portage on the seldom-traveled route from Ontario's Hematite Lake to Red Paint Lake. In the early-morning sunlight, fresh raindrops from the night before glistened from every twig, leaf, and needle and hung in sparkling geometric precision from trailside spiderwebs. Whispering Canada jays politely ushered us to the lakeshore where we pitched camp, went for a swim, and laundered a week's grime from our clothes. That evening, the gods of angling success provided a pair of lake trout that Lil broiled and served up in pink-meated splendor. And later, when the stars came out and crowded down to the treetops, we sat for a long time on the sand, soaking up the feeling of timelessness and reflecting that it is well for the soul to periodically depart from those complex centers of society where the human species is so frantically concerned with itself and to follow the canoe trails into the wild country where the sheer magnitude of land, water, and sky tends to restore the ego to more realistic proportions.

The first-time visitor to the canoe country invariably comments on the silence. But, in truth, there is no silence. It is simply that ears tuned to the off-time, discordant, hyped-up clatter of the city have difficulty adjusting to the rhythm and harmony orchestrated for the remote country. The obvious sounds are quickly identified— the vocal clamor of loons, gossiping in their backyards, the scolding cries of herring gulls as they bank and soar on translucent white pinions over their rocky nesting sites. But it takes more accurate tuning to sort out the members of that shoreline symphony, which includes insects, songbirds, and amphibians. With concentration, the soloists are discernible—crickets from the string section, chickadees, redwing blackbirds, and whitethroat sparrows representing the woodwinds, and frogs handling the brass. In time, the ear distinguishes the staccato drumroll of the downy woodpecker from the steady, four-four time of his big, pileated cousin. And even with the house lights extinguished, the outdoor theatergoer can discern the muffled rustling of whitetail deer, moving like well-trained ushers up the forest aisles.

How subtle are the differences in sound between wind stirring the leaves on birch or popple and that same wind sighing through the needles on white pine and Norway pine, or the rhythmic slapping of a breeze-stirred ripple against the shoreline in comparison to the relentless crash of gale-force waves. But these are only a few of the sounds.

The sights of the canoe country are staged on an even grander scale. How breathtaking is the huge backdrop, stretching from horizon to horizon, shifting by season from the pale gray of early spring to the deep green of midsummer, only to be replaced in the fall by broad brush strokes of scarlet, orange, russet and yellow before the final curtain comes down and the entire set is stored for the long winter under layers of white.

And finally, there are the great performances, the tragedies, the comedies, the tears, and the laughter. Who can fail to identify with the terror of a hunted deer as it turns, twists, and backtracks in a futile attempt to evade a closing wolf pack in full cry. Shift to the scene where a timid hare crosses a clearing at dusk, carefully looking to the right and left, but failing to note the silent shadow descending from overhead until too late, the needle-sharp talons of a great horned owl driving deep through hair and skin with lethal force.

Then switch to the circling bald eagle, the great politician of the remote country, who greedily observes the toiling osprey struggling home with his day's catch of trout—and then drops from the sky with a shriek to deprive the osprey of his fish, the eagle's due in taxes. There are the evening acrobats, the flying squirrels that glide soundlessly from branch to trunk, and fun-loving otters who try to outdo each other with aquatic gymnastics. The harried mother blackduck herds her brood swiftly along the shore as she attempts to take them through kindergarten to a high school diploma in survival in a few short weeks. The kingfisher, that wild-eyed, blue-and-white diving artist, plunges from his high perch headfirst into the water, emerging in full flight while he chatters his own applause.

These, then, are some of the elements, the fragments that are a part of canoeing, those experiences so unusual in each 24 hours that we can understand the Indian when he says, "Today I have lived a hundred years."

Friend, the fire has gone out and the night grows late. It is time to head to the tent, for tomorrow is a long day. Perhaps somewhere along the trail we will meet again. If you see our fire, paddle over and pull up your canoe. The coffee pot is always on.

Index

Wool sox, 161
World War I, 102
World War II, 83

Yarbro, Tom, 156
Zippers, repairing, 170–171; sleeping gear, 84